Where the
Hearth Is

Kate Humble

Where the Hearth Is

STORIES OF HOME

ASTER*

First published in Great Britain in 2023 by Aster, an imprint of
Octopus Publishing Group Ltd
Carmelite House
50 Victoria Embankment
London EC4Y 0DZ
www.octopusbooks.co.uk

An Hachette UK Company
www.hachette.co.uk

ISBN 978-1-78325-460-6

A CIP catalogue record for this book is available from the British Library.

Printed and bound in the United Kingdom

Typeset in 11.25/18.5pt Miller Text by Jouve (UK), Milton Keynes

10 9 8 7 6 5 4 3 2

Publisher: Stephanie Jackson
Creative Director: Jonathan Christie
Senior Editor: Alex Stetter
Production Managers: Lucy Carter and Nic Jones

Illustration: Melanie Lewis

This FSC® label means that materials used
for the product have been responsibly sourced.

Baggage. This one's for you.

Contents

———

Kansas or Oz?   1

The Snail   3

Childhood   7

The Pink Sofa   15

Sociable Weaver Birds   27

The Tattie Pan   33

The Pistol Shrimp and the Goby   43

A Garage Full of Trainers   47

The Swallow   57

Letters and Rings   61

Seeing Green   77

The First House   89

The Homing Pigeon   97

Dignity and Trees   101

The Cuckoo   113

A Long Walk   117

The Hermit Crab   131

CONTENTS

Where Is Home . . .?   135
. . . And What's Inside It?   145
The Bowerbird   157
A Stuffed Duck and Gold Teeth   163
Badgers   173
Kindness   179
The Man Who Fell from the Sky   193
The Hippos of Colombia   197
Carpets and Curtains   199
The Second House   215
Birds and Flowers   223
The Guillemot   233
Land and Sea   235
The Common Wasp   247
A Scottish Glen and Pieces of Blanket   251
The Echidna   261
Memories and Feelings   265
I'm Here   275

Author's Acknowledgements   287
Publisher's Acknowledgements   289
About the Author   291

Kansas or Oz?

———

Home: the word we use to refer to the place where we live. A simple, no-nonsense, everyone-knows-what-it-means sort of word. But contemplate it for a moment or two and it's not quite as straightforward as it seems. It's not the same as 'house', or 'flat', or 'camper van'. Those are words for things that if we were to be shown a picture of them, we would recognise for what they are. But 'home' is different. It is something more nebulous and intangible. It's not simply a structure with a door and a bed in it. It's more than that. Something infinitely more precious and hard-won.

Dorothy in *The Wizard of Oz* tells us 'There's no place like home', but what makes a home? What are its constituent parts? Why Kansas and not Oz? If we are homesick, what is it about the place we call home that is lacking elsewhere? Can you ever, truly, 'make yourself at home' – as kind hosts encourage – somewhere that isn't? Is 'home' a state of mind as much as a place, somewhere familiar and comfortable? Somewhere to be barefoot and barefaced? Where you can put your feet on the furniture; eat peanut butter straight from the jar with your finger; laugh, cry, retreat from the world? Is it the place – the only place – where you can feel entirely liberated, where you can truly be yourself? Where you feel safe?

Is home landscape? Is it people? Family? Belongings? Roots? History? Continuity? Is home always a fixed point, a known place, or can it be transient? Or is it a feeling? Something you carry with you wherever you go.

This book is the search for home: what it is and what it means. The stories in the pages that follow are all true. They are formed from conversations with people of different ages and circumstances, who each gave their own unique insight into what 'home' means for them. I turned to the natural world for inspiration and answers too. What – if any – sense of home do our wild compatriots have? It turns out, in many cases, to be as strong and as varied as ours. No surprise, perhaps, given that we are wildlife too.

To be invited over the threshold into someone's home is an extraordinary act of generosity and trust. I understand now, having stepped over so many thresholds in the writing of this book, that a home is the most private and cherished of spaces, one that isn't easily attained and can't just be found in an estate agent's window. And I thank everyone who gave me the great honour and courtesy of sharing their home with me.

The Snail

Beneath the kitchen window of my childhood home was a thick hedge growing up against the pebble dash. Its dense, dark brown twigs, completely hidden in spring by a glossy cloak of green leaves and pink blossoms, made it a perfect hiding place. Not for me – it grew too tight to the wall and was too scratchy to make it a den – but blackbirds always chose it to nest in. We would watch them from the window, darting in with thin twigs and bits of grass in their beaks and then, after a few days, I would creep quietly around the hedge, trying to spot the nest. Occasionally, I would see and catch the eye of the dark brown female, almost invisible in the protective gloom, just the brown-yellow of her beak giving her away. Sometimes she'd be off the nest, revealing the eggs, four or five of them, bright blue and speckled. It was like getting a glimpse of stolen treasure.

A delicate fragment of blue shell on the ground beneath the hedge was a clue that the eggs had hatched. Sure enough, we'd start to hear the hungry chirps of the chicks as their mother returned to their hideaway with a beak full of worms. Then the day would come when we'd see the fat little fledglings, gapes still yellow, perching slightly precariously on the outer branches of the hedge, waiting to make that great leap into adulthood.

Once they had gone, I could go back to my search for the other creatures that lived on the damp, shaded patch of wall behind the hedge. This was a favourite resting place for snails. Few gardeners are thrilled by the sight of snails, but my brother and I loved them. We would collect them and keep them in an old ice cream carton with holes punched in the lid. We'd line it with soil, put a bit of broken flowerpot in the corner for them to hide in and feed them lettuce. We'd use a dab of Mum's nail polish to mark their shells and spend happy hours at the weekend snail racing. Not a high-octane spectator sport, it's true – a snail's top speed is just over 1cm a second – but such was the innocence of 1970s childhoods that snail racing could easily be the most exciting thing that happened on a Saturday. Plus, snails were curious – almost alien – with eyes on stalks that they could retract at will and their ability to produce slime. And being gratifyingly easy to find and capture, and seemingly unbothered about being manhandled, meant we could while away happy hours in their company. The thing we admired about them most was their ability to disappear into their shells in a fraction of a second, then reappear when they felt so inclined. There was something enviable about that complete self-reliance: that whenever they felt the need to retreat to safety, all they had to do was a bit of muscular gymnastics and retract themselves into their portable shelter.

Snails are born with their shells, hatching from a clutch of small, white, circular eggs that are laid in a shallow hole in the ground dug by the adult. Snails are hermaphrodite – at a push they can self-fertilise, but would rather not. If they find a mate, which they do with the briefest of foreplay, each fertilises the eggs of the other, which, at a snail's customary pace of life, can take anything between four and twelve hours. Once they hatch, their newly born offspring will eat the eggs they have emerged from, absorbing the calcium they contain to harden up their soft, transparent shells. The shells grow with the snail, the whorls of the shell widening as the snail gets bigger, so it is always the perfect size and fit. And the whorls are always on the right-hand side of the shell, which allows mating to happen unimpeded. Although there are anomalies. A snail was once found in a garden in south-west London that had whorls on the left side of its shell. This is so rare, the finder deemed it worthy of study and sent it to a biologist at Nottingham University. The students named the snail Jeremy, after the left-leaning politician Jeremy Corbyn, and requested a nationwide search for another 'leftie' snail with which it could mate. They hoped this would help in their study of genetically inherited traits. A mate was found for Jeremy, but none of their offspring followed their parents' left-sidedness.

'The snail is the animal that carries its home on his back' is among one of the very first things we learn, along with 'E is for elephant'. But it is not strictly true. Snails are not, in fact, as footloose and fancy-free as we might imagine, happy to go, albeit slowly, wherever their mood takes them. Frustrated gardeners have long held suspicions that snails have the ability to come back, even after being tossed unceremoniously – and somewhat scurrilously – over a neighbour's fence. One woman became so convinced that the snails in her garden were not new intruders but animals that were familiar with the rich pickings to be had there that she challenged biologist Dave Hodgson at Exeter University to prove, scientifically, whether or not snails had some sort of homing instinct. And they do. Snails can find their way back to the place they consider their patch and have to be taken 20 metres or more away from it before they lose their bearings and fail to return. So gardeners have two choices: either to get better at throwing or to accept that to the snails they find there, their gardens are home.

Childhood

———

I was born in London but it was never home. Perhaps my parents had an inkling, even though I was barely six months old when we moved to the Berkshire countryside, that I wouldn't thrive in a city. Mum always joked that London wasn't big enough for me. Had I been born a couple of decades later, I may well have been described as 'hyperactive' or diagnosed with ADHD, but happily for me, I was never saddled with the burden of a formal condition that required dealing with. My parents' instincts were to give me space and freedom built on a solid foundation of stability. So my childhood was spent in a Victorian house, with rattly windows and uncertain plumbing, down a pot-holed stone track. It had a big garden, surrounded by the fields of the adjacent farm. We had neighbours, not immediately next door but all within walking distance. It wasn't a village, more what the French would describe as a *lieu-dit* – a small collection of houses that spread back from the bank of the River Thames. And we all knew each other. I have no doubt that the overwhelming feelings that accompany my memories of childhood – those of comfort and security – come as much from the people who lived around me as from my immediate family.

I remember them all still, even though I left that house over three decades ago and my parents sold it not long after I'd gone. It is the people, rather than the house, that I feel nostalgic for. Glamorous Sylv, who raced along the track like a rally driver in her gold Golf GTI and threw legendary parties. Rita, who had fled Germany in the war and now lived quietly with her friend Gisela. She gave me a kitten, a tiny bundle of tabby fur, for my second birthday and told me stories in her gently accented English while we ate the cinnamon biscuits she always had in a tin in her kitchen. She never told me about her past, I'm not sure she spoke of it to anyone, but it was present in an intangible way – in her eyes, in the way she held herself.

Rosemary was fiery, with long red curls and a sharp tongue, which perhaps accounted for her largely silent husband, Victor. But in the right mood, she was gruffly kind, if always a little scary. There was a huge mulberry tree in their garden and when the berries were ripe, we had an open invitation to go round and pick as many as we wanted. My brother and I would sit beneath its dark green canopy feasting on the sweet, fragrant berries, our fingers and tongues stained red-purple by the juice.

Rosemary had a horse, an enormous flea-bitten grey called Rush Hour. I think she liked horses rather more than she did people, so when, at the age of five, I developed a burgeoning obsession for horses myself, she did everything she could to encourage it, including hoisting me up on to Rush Hour's broad, bare back and leading me along the lane, laughing that I looked like 'a sparrow on the rock of Gibraltar!'.

Pat and Keith lived alongside the river, had two children a little younger than us and a boisterous, long-suffering Labrador. I was rather in awe of Keith, who worked in the music industry, had long hair, a pierced ear and wore T-shirts with the names of bands on. We'd go there sometimes after school and have tremendous water fights fuelled by cans of Coke and Sherbet Dib Dabs.

In sharp contrast were Maggie and Kit, both immaculately elegant and benevolently formal. A hug from Maggie would envelop you in a perfumed cloud of diaphanous florals. She always wore beautiful dresses, even in the wettest, muddiest depths of winter, and for my sixteenth birthday, gave me one too. It was her favourite colour – turquoise – and made of gossamer-thin layers of chiffon, light as air, a dress for Titania in *A Midsummer Night's Dream*. I suspect it was a gentle attempt to encourage me to be less of a tomboy, which, however much I loved Maggie, was not destined to happen. But I made up for it with my unbridled adoration of Bruin, their beloved golden retriever, who she would entrust to me for walks in the field across the lane from their house.

Our nearest neighbours, who lived on the opposite side of the track from us, were John and Joy. They had three freckly, fiercely clever children, a few years older than me, who were an endless source of fascination and discovery. They kept tadpoles in tanks and chrysalises in jars. They grew all sorts of exotic plants, like bananas, and every windowsill in the house was crowded with pots and seed trays. They had a piano and a small, noisy machine that transformed ordinary pebbles that we collected in the lane and from the gravel pit at the top into shining, smooth, gem-like treasures. John had built a swing that hung from the branches of a big tree behind the house and we would take turns to swing as high as we could, every part of our bodies straining, bare legs flung forward, propelling us up and up until it felt like we were flying.

It was this family who rescued us late one night when Mum heard a strange noise coming from upstairs. She opened the door of their bedroom to find the bed engulfed in flames. With great presence of mind, she shut the door, bundled me and my brother into blankets, scooped up the cat, and we made a mad dash in the dark, through the mud and the puddles to the safety of John and Joy's house. My hazy memories recall it being hugely exciting – an adventure rather than a trauma. We set up camp on the floor of their sitting room and Joy made us hot chocolate. Our house survived. We went over the following morning to find the firemen had heaved the burning mattress through the window; it lay in a sodden, still-steaming, black heap and everywhere smelt of smoke and wet soot. We couldn't move back for a week or so, but for my brother and me it didn't matter which house we were in. All of them were familiar enough to feel like home.

I left home when I left school. Bar those first few months of my life, my entire 18 years had been lived here, sleeping in a little single bed, tucked up under taut sheets and heavy blankets until duvets became a thing. When it was cold – and in winter the house was so cold there was often ice on the inside of the windows – we had hot water bottles and slept in jumpers and socks. Every spring, I'd witness the claret-coloured leaves of the cherry tree outside my bedroom window unfurl and watch pink-breasted bullfinches feast on the buds of its blossom. I knew the hedges and bushes where the blackbirds and robins nested and would peep in to count the eggs and spy on the chicks when they hatched. I walked, cycled, rode a horse down every lane and track and field for miles around.

On hot days, we'd play in the sprinkler and cycle down the towpath to the lock where the kiosk sold ice lollies for 10p. Or an unruly gang of us would ride bareback to the village, where a slipway led into the river and we'd ride into the dark waters of the Thames, holding fistfuls of mane as anchors, and swim with the horses. I climbed – and fell out of – every apple tree in our little orchard and gathered their fruits in the early autumn for apple crumble. I learned to chop wood and light a fire, and at weekends we'd toast crumpets and have mugs of tea while we watched *The Muppets*. On Christmas Eve, my brother and I would go with Dad to buy the Christmas tree, which we'd all help to decorate, battling to extricate the tinsel and tangled fairy lights from the playful claws of the cat. We'd hang the same stockings, year after year, over the fireplace, leave a mince pie and a glass of whisky, which never failed to be gone by Christmas morning.

If I was rooted anywhere, it was here. I knew nowhere else.

And yet I was consumed with wanderlust and a need for independence. I was as happy to leave the house, the community and the countryside that had made up my home, as I was living there. And when my parents sold up three years later, I felt no pang, no compunction to try to persuade them to stay. It had ceased to be my home. I've never seen it or been back to the area since.

Why was it that somewhere that offered the safety, security and familiarity that are the foundation stones of a happy home life was so easy to leave? By choice, I have nothing – no childhood toys, or pictures, or pieces of furniture – that I grew up with. So what, if anything, from those formative years helps shape my idea of home now?

It takes a heap o' livin' in a house t' make it home,
A heap o' sun an' shadder, an' ye sometimes have t' roam
Afore ye really 'preciate the things ye lef' behind,
An' hunger fer 'em somehow, with 'em allus on yer mind.
It don't make any differunce how rich ye get t' be,
How much yer chairs an' tables cost, how great yer luxury;
It ain't home t' ye, though it be the palace of a king,
Until somehow yer soul is sort o' wrapped round everything.

From 'Home' by Edgar Albert Guest

The Pink Sofa

I wasn't quite sure what to expect when I set off to find the Springhill Cohousing Community. I'm intrigued by the concept of cohousing, though not sure whether it is a wonderful idea or a terrible one. Not sure, if I'm honest, what cohousing really means. Is it the same as a commune? One of those infamous, hippie dens of iniquity from the 1960s, all tie-dye and free love and dope? Can you only eat chickpeas and sourdough and wear plastic shoes? Do you have to share everything?

I don't have anything against sharing. I like and applaud the idea of shared resources and of shared effort bringing shared reward, a community working together for the equal benefit of everyone – growing vegetables or tending an orchard, say. It also makes perfect sense to me for people to share things they may only use sporadically. I visited a community in Holland that had clubbed together to buy two electric cars and a number of bicycles that everyone could use when they needed. My local town has a Library of Things – garden equipment, tools, gazebos, tea urns – which we can borrow rather than having to go and buy them. Community shared agriculture schemes give people the opportunity to grow food for themselves and others, when they might not have the time, space or knowledge to do it by themselves.

But I fear the pettiness that I imagine can all too easily overwhelm the pleasures of communal living. I shudder at the thought of committees and rules and endless meetings. I don't want to be told what I can and can't do in my own home. I like having people around, but I also like – and need, very much sometimes – to be solitary.

My sat nav takes me down a very ordinary-looking residential street in the Gloucestershire town of Stroud, at the end of which an unobtrusive sign tells me I'm now entering the Springhill Cohousing Community. For some reason, I hadn't expected it to be within the town. I imagined it would be more separate, more exclusive feeling. Not in a 'posh' way, just in a more obvious 'we've chosen to live differently' sort of way. That there would be gates and almost certainly prayer flags. There are neither. I pull into an area where there are a few cars parked and the road ends. There is a blackboard in front of a parking space that has my name on with '12–2pm' written underneath. Standing next to it is a small, slim woman, hair in a ponytail, velvet coat, dangly earrings, holding a dog on a lead.

'I'm Jo,' she says as I get out of the car. 'And this is Peggy.' I give the dog a scratch behind the ear which she acknowledges with a wag of her perky tail. 'Visitor parking is one of the bugbears here. It's limited to two spaces, so it has to be booked in advance and

I had to guess how much time you might need. I hope a couple of hours is enough. Do you want to walk around first before we go and have a cup of tea?'

It's a rather grey November day, but even in the flat, wintery light, the exterior of the buildings, partly clad in wood, look inviting. There's a uniformity which gives a sense of cohesion, but enough variety in the buildings' design to avoid the look and feel of the characterless red-brick housing estates that are the feature of so many of the UK's residential suburbs. Jo points out the studio flats, each with a broad, generous balcony and parking beneath, but beyond where I've left my car, access to the rest of the community is only on foot. Paths run between the rows of houses, each with their own small gardens in front of wide, glass doors. There's a small, communal 'secret garden' with a little table set beneath apple trees and a very organised composting system. In the heart of the estate is a big open area of grass – the equivalent of a village green – with a climbing frame and a swing, and where, Jo tells me, they have events like the Springhill Day in the summer: 'Which I run because I love that sort of thing. We do egg and spoon races and people make cakes and cook; it's a great way for everyone to be part of the community and be together.'

A tall, angular building borders the green. 'That's the common house,' Jo tells me and leads me inside. There's a pool table and table tennis and beyond that the laundry. 'It's 30p a wash,' says Jo. 'It makes life so easy. I think about half the community use the laundry rather than having their own machines.'

Up the stairs, there is a big sitting room, with sofas and a piano and shelves of books residents can exchange, and on the floor above, a kitchen and dining room with big windows looking out over the whole site. Once a week, communal meals are prepared and served for the first 30 residents who sign up. A meal costs £4 and is cooked on a rota system by the residents.

'Each of us cooks once a month. It's my turn next week.'

'Are there other duties you have to do?' I ask.

'Each of us is responsible for a week, twice a year, for locking up the common house at night and there's a mowing rota for the communal gardens, which is just once a year.'

We walk together towards Jo's house. There are few other people about – it being the middle of a weekday – and it is so extraordinarily tranquil that I'm amazed, when we reach the lower part of the estate, to discover we really are right in the heart of Stroud: the town, visible through the trees that mark the boundary, is spread out below us and across the valley.

'I love Stroud,' Jo says, looking out fondly over the buildings. I've lived here for 42 years and wouldn't really want to go anywhere else now.'

Although she once imagined her life would be in Devon, where she trained in theatre at Dartington College of Arts. She met her husband, Greg, there and when they graduated, they had a plan to start a theatre company providing good, professional theatre to rural communities. But the Arts Council turned down their application for funding, saying there were already too many small-scale theatre companies in Devon and the south-west. 'But if you go to Gloucestershire . . .'

So Jo, Greg and fellow members of their troupe hitchhiked up the motorway, found a communal house to rent and started Dr Foster's Travelling Theatre. It wasn't long before they discovered Stroud and for Jo and Greg, it instantly felt special: 'It's beautiful, but feisty, with a history of political activism and a reputation as a centre for arts and music, so that's where the company settled.'

'Presumably you chose to live communally with the rest of your group because it was the practical thing to do financially and because you were all working together?' I ask.

'No, I chose to live like this because I love waking up in the morning and having people to interact with. It can be really, really annoying living with people, and it can be a bit student-ish, I know, but a friend of mine who lives alone now she's divorced expresses the feeling of living with others perfectly when she says, "It's about having someone moving the air around you."'

Jo and Greg bought a house in Stroud, home for them and their two daughters. Twenty years later, after they divorced and their daughters had left, Jo moved to Springhill. The community is built on six acres of land that had been bought by a man called David Michael in September 2000. It had been the site of a large house which had fallen into dereliction; the grounds were swamped by nettles and brambles. David's plans were inspired by the cohousing movement that had started in Denmark in the 1970s and has since gained worldwide popularity. With the help of Kathryn McCamant and Charles Durret's seminal book *Cohousing* and Christopher Alexander's

A Pattern Language, he set about creating the first new-build cohousing community in Britain.

Springhill follows a broad set of principles that many cohousing projects share – parking on the periphery leaving the main site free of cars being one of them. There are 35 homes – someone worked out that between 30 and 40 dwellings is the optimum number for a community – ranging from studio flats to five-bedroomed houses. They are self-contained, well-insulated, low polluting and energy saving. They are also entirely private and privately owned. They can be bought and sold, like any other house, although there is a service charge to cover the upkeep of communal spaces. Those communal spaces are intrinsic to the cohousing idea, giving residents the chance to meet regularly and eat together. It is, David believes, 'the way forward for human beings to live together in a safe, independent and caring neighbourhood'.

The first people moved in in 2003, when it was still, according to Jo, a building site: 'So they were slopping about in the mud and living higgledy-piggledy with each other until houses became finished.'

Jo moved in three years after Springhill was completed, encouraged by the people she now lives next door to, and has been here for 16 years. 'It was the perfect solution for me,' she says. 'It's different from a commune or a kibbutz. We have our own space but we are also very much part of a community. We live here because we want love and support and the fun and friendship of neighbours, who, by living here, have made the same choices.

They *want* to be neighbours and interact with people around them. That's why cohousing is also known as an "intentional community". It's a really good model. It's a really good way to live.'

But there are also aspects of life there that feel cumbersome, she concedes. 'There are a lot of emails. You have to spend a lot of time reading through discussions. There's a residents' meeting once a month and every fortnight there is a time for what we call "single-issue" meetings.'

'What kind of thing?'

'Well, someone wanted to paint the outside of their front door bright red. Now, you might think, "Oh god, I just want to paint my door red and yet I've got to ask everyone first. What a bloody cheek!" [That is *exactly* what I'm thinking.] But it is actually about respecting each other, listening to each other's opinions and concerns on issues that affect us all, even if it is something as trivial as having to walk past a bright red door every day. And although it can seem petty, and it can be frustrating at times, I like learning other perspectives and being encouraged to see things from another point of view.'

It doesn't work for everyone. Jo has seen plenty of people of all ages move to Springhill only to leave because they find consensual living too restrictive or exasperating.

'I find rules tricky too,' Jo admits, 'because I think every situation needs to be looked at as a one-off, but I do understand why we need them. I think of them more as guidelines, which makes it easier! Come on in.' She opens the door of her house and I follow her and Peggy inside.

The downstairs is dominated by an open plan kitchen and living room, flooded with light from the glass doors that open on to her garden. High ceilinged, bright and airy, it feels sleek and contemporary, but very much a home. Jo's vibrant nature, her love of theatre, art, books and family are immediately apparent. The white walls are adorned with photographs, doodles, paintings and posters. There's a wood burner, a bright pink sofa and a round table where we sit with our mugs of tea.

'I remember when I first moved in here,' Jo says. 'I was trying to get my music system to work and I just couldn't. So I sent out a tentative, slightly embarrassed email to the community to see if anyone could help. Within five minutes, there were three men at the door! There's huge comfort from living in a place that is based on the idea of intentional support, particularly for single people. Of course, you can still be lonely, but as an extrovert living here on my own, I know I can always go and knock on someone's door. And I've had a number of lodgers over the years, which I love.'

I noticed, when I first came in, the word 'home' painted in black and white letters on a piece of paper and tacked to the wall above the mirror.

'Oh, that's just one of my doodles. It's not a very beautiful piece of art but it's really important to me, that word.'

'What does it embody?'

'A place of absolute safety and security.'

Together, we look at the other things she has on the walls. There's a photo of her year group at Dartington College, all of them adopting self-conscious, thespy poses. There are paintings she's collected or been given by friends, photographs of Peggy when she was a puppy.

'My art, every painting I have, every photograph I have has a very, very strong connection with me. These are the things that make this house a home. I once went back to the house in Kent that I grew up in with my sister. The new family were very friendly, let us come in and showed us around, but I realised that without our stuff, it wasn't our home. It was just a building. I didn't feel emotionally connected to it at all.' She rests her hand on the back of the pink sofa. 'This is special too. It's not an heirloom or anything, but about the time that Greg and I got divorced, I inherited a bit of money and I thought, "Right, I'm going to buy a really comfy sofa." My daughter Jess came with me. We decided we wanted one with arms you could rest your head on without knocking yourself out and for it to be long enough for both of us. When I got it, it became the place we would both go when we needed a big cuddle. We call it "going on the pink". So, if Jess spots that I'm feeling a bit low, she'll say, "Come on Mum! On the pink!"'

She pauses for a moment then points to another photo. 'That's my other daughter Harry,' she says. 'And there she is with shorter hair.' I look at the beautiful face of a young woman with a thick tumble of chestnut brown hair. In the other, her hair is short and she's wearing a quirky little black and white hat. She is surrounded by friends. You can almost hear their laughter. Harry's face is full of life and full of hope, even though, at that moment, she was dying.

Harry had been diagnosed with spinal cancer. After a spell of treatment and rehab at Stoke Mandeville Hospital, she moved in with her mum. She was in a wheelchair, so Jo made a bedroom and bathroom for her on the ground floor of her house, but the garden beyond the sliding doors of the living room was then just a grassy slope, not navigable by wheelchair.

'I put out an email to the community and within a week, they had made Harry a tarmac path through the garden so she could go anywhere she wanted on site. She loved having a bath but mine is upstairs, so Anne, over the road, let her use hers. And there was always someone to help me lift her. Harry summed it up perfectly. She said, "Mum, I feel so safe here because, say you weren't here and I fell out of this wheelchair, I've got 34 numbers on the phone I can ring and I know someone will come."'

Harry died in 2012. Her funeral was held at the nearby community arts centre in Stroud.

'I was worrying about providing tea for everyone who wanted to come, but the Springhill community said, "We'll do it in the Common House. We'll do the food. We'll do everything!" Harry loved flowers, but she also had strong environmental views and would not have wanted the room full of cut, hothouse flowers. So one of the garden group at Springhill said "I've got an idea!" And they dug up snowdrops from the garden, put them in brown ceramic pots. After the wake was over, the flowers went back in the earth. It was just perfect.' Her eyes fill with tears. 'They did an amazing spread of food. The room looked beautiful, exactly as Harry would have wanted, and they looked after everything.

I didn't have to be a host, I could just hunker down with her friends and her father. Those acts of empathy, and intelligence and kindness, they really matter. Their support was absolutely incredible.'

'Will you stay here now, do you think?' I ask.

'I think so,' Jo says. 'I'm deeply woven into Stroud life. I co-run the annual Stroud Film Festival. I've run the youth theatre here for 27 years. Everyone knows me. When I walk down the street, people say "Hi Jo!" The only reason I'd leave is if my daughter Jess and her children moved somewhere that I couldn't get to from here easily. But I'm hoping they might come and live here.'

She walks back with me to the car. It is past 2pm – I've overstayed my allotted time – and I've been parked in by another car. Jo and I laugh. 'Bloody rules!' There's a note on the windscreen of the car blocking me, saying which house they are in. 'I don't think we need to disturb them, do we?' I say to Jo. And she gives me a conspiratorial nod. Together we shift plant pots, a garden table and chairs and, with a bit of back and forth, I manage to squeeze the car out of the gap. We put everything back and hug.

'Thank you!' I say. 'It's a special place, this.' She gives a slight nod of assent and waves me off.

Sociable Weaver Birds

When humans first started to build shelters – and the earliest
remnants found that were indisputably once homes date from
400,000 years ago – they might well have looked for inspiration
from the animals around them. The way sociable weaver birds
live, and how they construct their nests, could have been a
template for some of the first human settlements. And it would
have been a good example to follow.

Throughout the Kalahari and Namib deserts of southern
Africa, tall, smooth-barked trees and telegraph poles will often
be adorned by large shaggy structures built high off the ground,
using the strong upright support they provide. These structures,
that resemble slightly unruly haystacks, are made with a roof of
tough twigs thatched with thick stems of grass. That same grass
is used to create a series of chambers, each with their own
entrance, accessed from underneath, protecting them from the
weather and making it hard for predators to break in. Each
chamber is lined with softer plant material, feathers or fur, and

is home to one pair of weavers. A sociable weaver bird nest can be made up of over a hundred of these chambers, be as much as six metres wide, three metres tall and weigh over a tonne.

But the nests aren't just used for breeding and abandoned, as most birds' nests are after the chicks have fledged. Weaver birds stay put and their offspring often do too. Some will never leave the nest, moving into empty chambers near their parents or adding a new one on to the side of the structure. And the communal living goes beyond simply sharing a roof. The birds share duties too. Adult birds will bring food for chicks that are not their own. When chicks fledge, they will be fed by juveniles in the colony until they are confident and able to feed themselves.

When not breeding, the weaver birds use the nest as a roost throughout the rest of the year, its construction offering climate-controlled respite from the desert extremes of temperature. Chambers will be refurbished and re-used by successive generations, often for more than a century.

The weavers' sociability even goes beyond their own species. Other species of bird are allowed to join the colony and nest there too, including – perhaps overgenerously – the pygmy falcon. This tiny bird of prey, the smallest in the region, doesn't build a nest of its own. Instead, it relies entirely on the generosity of the weaver birds, exclusively laying its eggs, brooding and raising its chicks in one of the chambers within their colony. A big ask from a predator that hunts and feeds on small birds. As acknowledgement, perhaps, of the safe haven the colony offers, pygmy falcons will only rarely attack a sociable weaver. And the advantage of having these other species in their midst is collaboration: learning from each other where there are sources of food, offering each other protection, having more eyes and ears listening out for danger. For a sociable weaver bird, home and community are one and the same. Without their community they have no home.

Here sparrows build upon the trees,
And stock-dove hides her nest:
The leaves are winnowed by the breeze
Into a calmer rest;
The black-cap's song was very sweet;
That used the rose to kiss;
It made the paradise complete:
My early home was this.

The redbreast from the sweetbrier bush
Dropt down to pick the worm;
On the horse-chestnut sang the thrush,
O'er the house where I was born.
The moonlight, like a shower of pearls,
Fell o'er this 'bower of bliss',
And on the bench sat boys and girls:
My early home was this.

The old house stooped just like a cave,
Thatched o'er with mosses green;
Winter around the walls would rave,
But all was calm within;
The trees are here all green again,
Here bees the flowers still kiss,
But flowers and trees seemed sweeter then:
My early home was this.

'My Early Home' by John Clare

The Tattie Pan

———

A storm blows in from the sea, a fury of wind and rain. The sky booms and crackles. Sharp flashes of white light illuminate, just for an instant, a landscape resistant and stoic, well-used to the onslaught of this sort of weather.

The old buildings are used to it too. The solidly built stone croft – a neat, two-storey rectangle, reminiscent of a child's drawing, cosied up with its byres and sheds in the lee of the hill – has weathered over 150 years of winter storms like this one.

Inside, tucked into their beds, are Ruby and Willie Brown. It is early still – barely seven in the morning – and what better way to let the storm pass than safe beneath the blankets in the house that has sheltered you all your life?

For this is the house where Ruby and Willie were born – not quite a year apart – Ruby in 1946 and Willie in 1947, ten days shy of Ruby's first birthday. It was where their father had grown up, having moved to this remote valley on the west coast of Shetland with his mother and siblings in 1922. Like most crofters, even today, they were tenants, but tenancies in Shetland frequently get passed down to the next generation. Willie and Ruby's father took over the croft from his mother. When he married, he stayed in his childhood home; his wife moved in and together they continued to work the land, growing tatties and rearing sheep.

Their children went to the local primary school but had to go away to Shetland's capital, Lerwick, for secondary school. Willie didn't enjoy education; he struggled, he says, to keep up and do the homework, and hated being away from his home. He left as soon as he was allowed and, at 15, returned to the croft to work with his father. But Ruby stayed on at school, coming home at weekends. 'Except sometimes in the winter when there was snow and the road was blocked,' Willie remembers, laughing. 'When she couldn't get home, she was like a bear with a sore head.'

And although she had to leave Shetland to go to university in Aberdeen, and again to do her teacher training in Edinburgh, Ruby came home every holiday, even once she was working. 'I don't think I ever missed the chance to come back to Shetland,' she says. 'It didn't matter where I was living – Shetland was always home. It was family, the place I'd grown up. Being with your folks and everything you know.'

Willie wonders whether their primary school teacher had a lasting influence on Ruby's deep-rooted sense of where she belongs. 'She was very interested in nature and was always encouraging us to explore the beach, gather wildflowers, that sort of thing. It made us feel very connected to what was around us and to appreciate it. Maybe that's what drove Ruby to keep coming back: everything was recognisable and familiar.'

Ruby returned to live in the Shetland croft in 1976 to care for their father in the last months of his life. When he died, she stayed on to support their mother. She was offered a job teaching in the local village and never considered getting a house of her own. Home was the house she grew up in, with the people she had grown up with. And even after their mother died in 1993, when she could have gone anywhere, she stayed on at the croft. 'Our parents weren't there, but the land was there. If you're a crofter – born into crofting – you're nowhere without the land. It doesn't matter that it is rented and not owned, it still needs looking after and there is still pride in raising good stock on it.' And as neither Ruby nor Willie had married, it made perfect sense for them both to continue living in the house that was to be home to the Brown family for almost 100 years.

The morning of the storm, Willie heard a bang. 'I thought it was thunder but it didn't sound quite right – it didn't rumble away, like thunder does. And there was a hot wire smell. I had an old heater in my bedroom that I'd left on – a very old-fashioned sort of thing – and I thought maybe it was the wiring downstairs that was connected to it which had overheated. So I put on a shirt and trousers and opened my bedroom door. The landing was full of smoke. I went downstairs, opened Ruby's bedroom door, shouted, "You have to get up!" The fuse board is in the porch. I opened the door and it was burning, dropping bits onto some plastic tubs on the floor beneath, and they were burning. There were some old mops in the corner, so I hauled them out, hoping that would reduce the smoke. But there was no sign of Ruby and I was calling her and calling her and there was no response. "Oh god!" I was thinking. "Oh no . . .'"

Ruby had pulled a jumper on over her pyjamas, opened her bedroom door and the room immediately filled up with smoke. There were flames in the hall now, blocking her way to the porch. Her only way out was through her bedroom window, but she couldn't get it open. Willie heard a noise behind him, looked back and saw Ruby through the glass, struggling with the window catch. From the outside, he too worked to force the window open and between them they finally managed to lift the sash high enough for Ruby to squeeze out. 'Thank goodness I'd had my hip done,' she says, quietly, 'because I don't think I'd have managed otherwise.'

Their house had been struck by lightning. The phone was dead and there was no mobile signal in the valley. Willie, through force of habit, had put the keys to his truck in his pocket when he locked it the night before. They had to drive to the main road – over two miles away – before they had enough signal to alert the fire brigade. As they started back down the hill, they could see their home. 'It was blazing.' They just sat in the truck on the road, not moving, hardly able to think. 'It was shock,' says Ruby, 'absolute shock.'

An ambulance came soon after the fire engines and took Ruby and Willie to hospital in Lerwick to check them over. Willie was kept in overnight. Ruby was discharged and stayed with a cousin. Willie had left the house in his shirt and trousers and slippers, with the keys to his truck but without his glasses. Ruby, in her jumper and pyjamas, had her glasses but nothing else. When they returned to the house, the four stone walls still stood, but the roof and everything inside was gone. All that was recognisable, in the smouldering drifts of ash and rubble that covered the ground floor, were scattered mattress springs and the singed hulk of Ruby's beloved Rayburn stove. But everything else – a century of the Brown family history – had been consumed by the flames and lost forever.

Willie meets me at the gate. He's a tall, gangly figure, but with the sort of wiry physicality that comes from a life working the land. Between his unruly head of white hair and equally unruly white beard he has kind, lively eyes in a face tanned and weathered by decades of outdoor labour. He leads me through to the kitchen, where Ruby is clicking on the kettle and getting mugs out of the cupboard. In contrast to her brother, she is neat and compact, with thick, straight grey hair, cut short, everything tucked in, a practical bustle about her. I imagine her in a classroom and something about her manner reminds me of a teacher at my primary school. Mrs Holt was fierce – actually quite scary – but inspired everyone she taught to do better than they thought they were capable of. I never had a finer teacher. I imagine Ruby was the same.

We sit at the table in the window. The room has an air of

impermanence. It is, undeniably, a kitchen, with everything in it you'd expect, but something intangible is missing. Kitchens are often the heart of a rural house, the modern equivalent of the medieval hall. Houses in the Middle Ages weren't split up into a series of rooms, each with its own designated purpose, like our houses today. Instead, there was one main room – the hall – where everything happened. It was a place of work, a place to cook, eat and sleep, all centred around the hearth which provided warmth and the means to cook.

I once stayed for a few days in a house that functioned in this way. It was on a small farm high up in the Andes mountains of Peru – a high altitude equivalent of Ruby and Willie's croft. The house was rectangular, built of solid mud bricks, with a compacted earth floor and a tin roof. It was lived in by Alejandrina and her husband and at one end of its single interior space was their bed, under which lived the family's guinea pigs – very much not pets but a valued supply of food in a harsh and difficult climate. At the other end was a large hearth, shaped from clay and moulded against the wall. There was a cave-like fireplace, big enough to hang a pot or a kettle above the coals, and alongside it, cubby holes had been scooped out of the clay for storing utensils and tins and jars of ingredients. The cubby holes closest to the fire would get warm from the heat, much to the delight of the cats, who, when not out stalking mice, would be found, particularly on cold mornings, curled up in them. In the space between the bed and hearth was Alejandrina's loom, tools and farm implements propped against the wall, storage boxes and a few rudimentary bits of furniture – a bench and a couple of wooden chairs that would be pulled out into the room when needed. But for all its practicality, it felt homely. I loved sitting on the floor by the hearth, Alejandrina and her daughter-in-law at their looms, the children playing, their father strumming a guitar. Evenings of stories and music and the crackle and glow of the fire.

Although not the sole room in the house, my farming friends' kitchens are, like Alejandrina's hearth, the pivotal point around which the family gathers and almost certainly where they spend most of their time when indoors. And although a kitchen is a much more 'public' space than, say, a bedroom or even a sitting room, it is this space, I think, that reflects the personal life of a family more than any other. Perhaps because it is often the first room you come into from the outside, it remains that medieval-style multi-use space.

More often than not, there will be a hammer or a wrench on the dresser alongside the crockery, bits of tractor on the kitchen table alongside a pile of farm paperwork, a basket of eggs and a cake tin. A dog will be asleep under the table, a cat curled up on a chair, wellies by the door, a coat on a hook, baler twine spilling out of the pocket. There's a pot on the stove, an almost permanently boiling kettle and old mugs in the sink. There are photos, usually of cattle or sheep winning prizes at agricultural shows; rosettes tacked to a cupboard door; a calendar on the wall, a free gift from the local feed merchant, its pages curled by the steam of the cooker. Walk into a kitchen like this and you can't help feeling like part of the family. The Germans have a word for this – *stimmung*. It translates, simply, as 'atmosphere': the feeling you get when you walk into a room.

This kitchen, in the house where Ruby and Willie are living as a stopgap, has all the practical things, but none of the things that made Ruby's own kitchen quintessentially hers. And it is the loss of her kitchen that causes her to feel particularly uprooted. 'I feel in limbo a lot of the time because I haven't got the things I would use every day. You go to boil the tatties, for example, and it's not your own tattie pan. Or you go for the knife that you like to chop the onions, and it's not there and it never will be. Or you want to cook a stew and you grab your pan and you just know what to do. Now I'm having to get used to someone else's kitchen, having to think more about doing things I used to do without thinking. And I miss my Rayburn stove,' she adds, with a small, fragile laugh. 'But I'm not ungrateful, please don't think that.'

'It's been so humbling,' Willie says, 'everyone's kindness . . .'

Once word got around about the fire, the response from their community was immediate. Someone offered their holiday let for them to stay in until something more permanent could be arranged – 'And we had streams of visitors with provisions, clothes and money.' All their ID had been lost – birth certificates and driving licences, as well as bank cards – but the bank in Lerwick, having looked after the Brown family all their lives, was able to order them new cards and give them access to their accounts.

A couple of months after the fire, a neighbour offered them this house. It is a pretty single-storey building on a quiet lane looking down over the inlet and the beach and close to their old croft. It is a lovely place to live but it's not, nor will it ever be, Ruby and Willie's home. Sitting with them in the kitchen I start to realise what is missing. There is nothing here that connects the house with Ruby and Willie. It's just a building – a roof and four walls – a practical solution to a problem. And that's how they see it. This house has no *stimmung* because it is not somewhere Ruby and Willie are, or will become, emotionally attached to. Their emotional attachment is all invested in their croft.

They go back every day. It's been less than six months since the fire and the experience is still raw. 'I feel sad every time I see the house,' says Willie, 'I wish we could just turn back the clock.'

'Yes, but it is also a reminder of how thankful we are that we were able to get out of it alive,' says Ruby. She's equally pragmatic about the possessions they lost. Willie mourns the books and the photographs, and Ruby the things she valued because they belonged to their parents – 'But then I realised they wouldn't care about those things as long as we were OK!'

They are still unsure what they will do. Rebuilding would need planning permission and take lots of time. 'We're not getting any younger . . .' But they are both insistent. They will go back. 'We need somewhere we can say is ours, whether its prefab or not,' says Ruby.

'The site is still home,' Willie adds. 'We miss the view. We've seen that all our lives and we miss it.'

The Pistol Shrimp and the Goby

_____

I will never forget the sensation of walking into that warm, clear water until it was over my knees. Then turning, lying back, face to the sky, kicking the long fins encasing my feet, watching the shore recede until our guide raised his hand, thumb and index finger joined to form a circle. Were we OK? We signalled back, OK! He gave the thumbs down sign that was our cue to let the air out of our buoyancy aids and sink beneath the blue, sunlit surface of the Red Sea.

Until this moment, I had never dived in tropical waters. Never experienced the sensory wonder of so much light and colour and life. I was visually accosted from every angle: above and below me the plants and animals of this strange marine world beckoned, each demanding my attention, and, naturally perhaps, my eyes were drawn to the big and the garish and the strange. We swam through the water slowly, barely moving at all. This tactic not only means a diver uses less air, so can stay in this underwater wonderland for longer, but also allows the little things – small treasures that get overlooked when overshadowed by the showier and more obvious – to catch the eye.

We drifted over an open patch of the seabed, bright with the dancing patterns cast by the rays of the sun through the water. I paused, alerted by a movement in the sand below me. Something unseen was digging, throwing a shower of grains up into the water. A small fish darted towards the spot, disappeared for a moment, then, as the grains settled and the water cleared, I saw the fish appear once again, emerging from the entrance of a newly dug burrow. It stayed there, just outside, seeming to look in my direction, but remained motionless. So did I. Moments later, a shrimp, small but with powerful front claws and long, waving antennae, emerged from the same burrow and rested in the sand right next to the fish. Two old friends, sitting on their porch, watching the world go by.

What I was seeing had also been spotted by a young marine scientist when he was diving in the Red Sea in 1957. Intrigued by these two entirely different creatures apparently sharing the same home, he caught the fish and the shrimp and put them in a tank in his lab to observe them. Sure enough, the pair stuck resolutely together, the shrimp digging a burrow for them to share in the sand at the bottom of the tank.

The shrimp is a pistol shrimp, an animal that excels at digging. Its constant excavations of the seabed not only provide it with a meal, dislodging tasty micro-organisms for it to feast on between digs, but also a safe place to hide from predators. But it has a problem: its eyesight. Which is so bad it can't see a predator coming until it's too late. But luckily, it has a lifelong friend to keep an eye out for any danger: the fish.

The fish is a goby. It formed its partnership with the shrimp back when they were juveniles and they have been together ever since. In return for being allowed to share the shrimp's burrow, the goby acts as security guard, always emerging first and waiting at the entrance. If the fish stays put, the shrimp will tentatively emerge too and stand right next to his partner, resting his sensitive antennae on the goby's body. Fish, as far as I'm aware, can't shout, but at the first sign of danger, the goby will release a chemical cue that the shrimp picks up with its antennae and both bolt back into their shared burrow and to safety.

A Garage Full of Trainers

He grew up in the Yorkshire Dales. James Herriot country. An old family farmhouse, with a barometer on the wall and a big kitchen table around which the family would gather every mealtime. His father was a farmer, as his father had been, and his father before that. His brother was following in his father's footsteps, but Barry couldn't imagine spending the rest of his life there. He knew it was a beautiful place to live, yet he was desperate to leave.

'I don't really understand why. I never saw or knew anything else other than that way of life, yet it never occurred to me to follow in my brother or my father's footsteps. I can't think back and identify a moment – a conversation, or a person I met, or a book I read – that made me feel differently from them. It was almost as if the most obvious option for me was just not an option. There was absolutely nothing wrong with where or how I grew up. I was just conscious that there was the rest of the world to discover.'

Barry was the first member of his family to go to university and one of the few members of his community to leave the area. Even now, in his fifties, he says that almost everyone he went to school with still lives within a ten-mile radius of the school gates.

Once he left home for a series of rented rooms and shared flats, he began to have a sense of creating a means of feeling at home wherever he was. It didn't take much – a few posters, books, music, plants, an ornament or two. Even when he left university and rented his first place as a professional care worker, he kept things simple, mainly due to a lack of money. 'I couldn't afford a bed and a mattress, so I made do with just a mattress, which seemed the most important thing. But I remember getting things like my first iron, my first vacuum cleaner, and thinking that having those domestic bits made the place feel somehow more homely.'

He continued his studies, training to be a social worker, and when he qualified and got his first job, he bought his first house, in Grimsby. He conceded that he would probably have continued to live in it in quite a spartan and simple way. But his partner at the time was what Barry described as 'incredibly homey. He had a very strong sense of how a home should be. It was really important to him that everything looked nice. That things matched.'

Together, they moved to a bigger house, one that was described in the estate agent's spec as 'an incredible house for parties'. A strange choice for Barry, who describes himself as an introvert. 'It was enormous. A great big living room and kitchen and summer room.' But they didn't entertain. For Barry's partner, it was a space to create a home for them both, not to show off to anyone else. And Barry was happy there. 'I went along with it! And I did feel at home there.' But when their relationship ended and Barry stayed on in the house, he became conscious of its size, that it was 'ridiculously big for one person'. But perhaps even more fundamental than the breakup was a trip he took soon afterwards to India. It was there he had an epiphany that made him re-evaluate everything. 'Why do we have so much stuff? We've only got two feet, so why do we have so many pairs of shoes? Why do we have all these clothes that we never get around to wearing? After that trip, my whole outlook on life was different.'

He sold the house on his return, bought a house that was a third of the size of his previous home and made him mortgage free. It needed work, so he spent time renovating it and in so doing found that he had given himself the opportunity to realise his childhood desire to discover more of the world. 'I had always had a plan to travel once I retired. I would work until I was 60, I thought, and then go. I began to wonder if I could do it a bit earlier – at 55, say. But then I realised, I could just rent out this house and see what adventures could follow.'

But there was someone else in Barry's life, a man sharing his house who he describes as his polar opposite. 'We're incredibly different personalities. Like two weird jigsaw pieces that strangely fit together.' Wayne is as flamboyant and talkative as Barry is understated and quiet. And their differences go beyond personality.

'The first thing I noticed about Barry's house was that there was nothing in it,' laughs Wayne. 'So I filled it!'

'Go on,' says Barry, 'tell her how many pairs of trainers you have.' He's deadpan but his eyes are twinkling.

'Over 200!' shrieks Wayne, delightedly.

'And how many hats?'

'Hats! Well, again, 100, maybe 200!'

'And even though you've only got two wrists, how many watches?'

'About a hundred!'

Barry shakes his head, fondly.

'I did kinda take over with my stuff,' Wayne concedes, 'but we balance each other out.'

Two years into their relationship, Barry came to a crunch point in his career. He had become quite senior in the organisation he was working for and loved his job. But the next step would have been to become a chief executive and he didn't feel that it was what he wanted to do. So he and Wayne started to think about going travelling together and when they might do it. The more they talked about it, the more they thought they should just get on with it. Not only that, they decided to do it by boat, undaunted by the fact that neither of them knew how to sail.

'We did a three-month sailing course,' Barry tells me.

'And went on a sailing holiday to Greece,' Wayne adds.

'And then set off around the world?' I ask, jokingly.

They both nod. 'Yes!'

It all started as a bit of a joke between them. 'We're going to sail around the world!' they'd laugh to each other, but the idea gathered momentum and almost before they realised what was happening, Barry had given up work, they'd rented out the house and become the proud owners of a boat. Not an ocean-going motor cruiser or superyacht, but a 13-metre, plastic-hulled sailing boat with one main living space and two other small cabins. They had enough money, they reckoned, to last them two years. This boat would not only be their means of seeing the world; it would be home. Their permanent home, even after their journey was over. Because neither of them wanted to think that this was going to be an adventure with an end, that they would return to the UK and normal life with nine-to-five jobs would resume.

For Barry, with his minimalist tendencies, deciding what to take was easy, the process of getting rid of things cathartic. 'My criteria for keeping something was did it have financial value, strong sentimental value or practical value. If it didn't, I got rid of it.' The stuff they could actually take with them had to be functional, had to earn its place on the boat. There could be nothing ornamental, nothing breakable. Everything they took had to be able to be stowed in the one cupboard when they were sailing. Which meant that Wayne had to leave almost everything behind.

'We stored our stuff in the garage of the house. Barry has almost nothing in there, he got rid of so much, whereas I couldn't just throw or give things away. My entire life is in boxes, piled floor to ceiling. Trainers, hats, belts, shoes . . .'

They set sail from Falmouth in 2015. Their boat proved not to be quite as seaworthy as they hoped and their route became somewhat dictated by the need to find places for its various problems to be fixed, which meant they missed out on some of the things they wanted to see and got through their money faster than they had planned. So they stopped in New Zealand, hoping to be able to work there to replenish their funds. They loved it.

Barry recalls, 'It was different enough to be exotic and exciting, but similar enough to home to feel you could fit in. There were other places we visited that, although beautiful and wonderful, made me realise that, even if I stayed there forever, I'd always be an outsider.' But they weren't allowed to work. They managed to stay for six months, living as cheaply as they possibly could, but knew it was only so long before they entirely ran out of money. They had to head back to the UK.

They were at sea for almost three years. Barry, the self-confessed minimalist introvert, never felt a pang of homesickness, never once felt constrained by life on a very small craft entirely surrounded by water. Wayne only started to feel the pull of home once they had decided that was where they were heading. 'Then I just wanted to be back. Back to what was familiar and to be able to meet up with people again. It was like that post-holiday feeling when you've had a good time but you realise you're ready for your own bed and a proper cup of tea!'

They returned to Falmouth, sailing in from the west, having circumnavigated the whole world. Barry's overwhelming sense of achievement was matched by the certainty that he wasn't done with sailing, that the adventure wasn't over. He just needed to make the money to enable him to set sail again, and the UK was the best place for him to do that. His return was purely practical, not emotional. And to ensure that he didn't slip back into the life he'd had before, he took the advice of some New Zealanders they had met who had been living on their boat and cruising the world for 15 years. 'Whatever you do,' they told him, 'don't park your boat in a marina and move back into a house because all your focus will be on the house and you'll forget about the boat.'

Barry and Wayne have been back in the UK for five years. They didn't move back into their house, nor, perhaps more tellingly, have they returned to the garage where they stored all the stuff they couldn't quite bear to part with. 'All the stuff I got rid of before we left, I haven't missed any of it,' Barry says. 'I couldn't even tell you what it was and if I went back to that garage now, I think I'd be surprised by what's there. It's nothing that I've ever needed and even things that I thought were of sentimental value are not things I long to see again.'

They continue to live on their boat, even through the years of the pandemic, when lockdowns meant they were confined to its one small living space. 'We literally lived around the table,' Wayne tells me. 'We sat at it for weeks on end. We couldn't go anywhere. In the end, we had to replace the foam in the seat cushions because we wore them out!'

But even being trapped in that tiny space didn't make either of them yearn to go back to a house. There are downsides, they tell me, and life isn't as liberating as people imagine. You can't just go where you want, when you want and for as long as you want.

There are restrictions and regulations and paperwork. And there are other considerations which can hamper a nomadic lifestyle at sea, not least the weather. Barry explains, 'That's the one thing the boat has in common with my childhood home: I have a barometer and it is as crucial to life at sea as it is to life on the land.'

Even when they are in a marina, the boat moored up and stationary in its berth, it doesn't work like a house. The bathrooms are several minutes' walk away. Mould and mildew cover everything in the winter. There is the worry that if bad weather hits when they are away visiting friends, the boat might get damaged or sink. 'And it isn't the same feeling returning to a house that is your home,' concedes Barry. 'It's not the same warm, emotional attachment. More of a relief that it's OK and still floating. We worry about the boat in a way we never did with the house.'

They've moved the boat a couple of times since they've been back and are currently moored at a marina on the west coast of Scotland. Waking up at anchor with a view of the Scottish Highlands, when a seal swims past while they are having breakfast or a pod of dolphins appears off the bow, are things that make life on a boat better than it could ever be in a house, they tell me. And it suits them, suits both their characters, even though they are so different. Barry always found the strong community he grew up in oppressive; being part of village life where everyone knew everyone made him feel uncomfortable. Even when he was older and chose to buy a house in a village, with every intention of engaging with the community, he admits he never did, which is why he thinks the itinerant lifestyle works for him. 'We can arrive at a marina and I can walk down the pontoon, nod and smile and say hello, but there is no need for it to go further than that. And it's a life that fits with my desire not to have stuff, not to conform. I don't want to go back to living in a house, having a nine-to-five job. I don't want a "normal" life. I like living differently. I like the alternative lifestyle; I like the simplicity of it.'

And the itinerant life suits Wayne's gregarious nature because there are always new people to meet, to talk to, to make friends with. 'The marina we're in now, we've only been in a month, but I've made friends with about 12 people. So home now, for me, is wherever we drop anchor. And wherever he is!' He gives Barry a cheeky smile. 'We're sea gypsies, now, aren't we?'

The Swallow

There you are!

It's a sense of movement. Peripheral. A feeling – rather than a seeing – that makes me turn my face to the sky. My eyes scan the blue-grey space, that clutching sensation of hope making my fists close around my thumbs. It is late April, not summer yet, but that wayward season that has you one day rolling up your shirt sleeves and basking in the sun's delicious warmth, and the next pulling on waterproof trousers and trying to remember where you've put your woolly hat. But summer *is* on the way, I think, as I smile a wide, delighted smile, because you're here. And the swallow flashes past, a dark streak and white flash, disappearing into the shadows cast by the eaves of the barn.

I know this bird. Know, even from that momentary glimpse of the long, thin, forked streamers of its tail, that it's a male. And I know it is likely that this male swallow hasn't just happened across my barn in my field. He has been aiming for this spot ever since he left the reed beds in South Africa where he spent the winter. Over the last six weeks, he has travelled over mountains and deserts and sea, flying a distance of 6,000 miles to get here. To get to my barn. Because he knows that tucked beneath the corrugation of the roof, wedged on the beam that holds the roof aloft, above the spot where the pig sleeps, is a nest. How does he know this? How did he know how to get here?

Dan Webb studies the swallows that nest in the barn at his mother's house. Every summer he puts a brightly coloured, lightweight ring on the leg of each of the chicks that have hatched and are ready to fledge. When the chicks, still with their clown-like gapes, are so big they crowd the nest, overhanging the sides, they know that soon there will be no choice: they will have to leap or be pushed. The rings are engraved with a code that is unique to each bird and Dan keeps careful records so he knows which birds were born in which nest and which ones make it back successfully from their winter migration. And what he has discovered is that the males born in the barn at his mother's house will invariably be the males he sees returning to breed there in subsequent years.

They find their way back with such unerring accuracy thanks to what they do after they fledge. The weeks before the weather and the shortening days trigger the move to start their long journey south are spent learning about their birthplace and their patch. They don't get this information from their parents – they may well be occupied raising a second brood or have started their migration already. The fledglings have to discover for themselves where the best sources of food are and how far they are from the nest; the places that aren't safe, where there might be predators. And most importantly of all, they have to gather a mental library of visual clues that will tell them they're back at the same spot.

Why do they bother? Why go to all the effort when surely any barn, any quiet, tucked away space will do? 'You feel comfortable in your own house because you know what should be where. It's the same for swallows. If they can return to a place where they know they can find food, where they know how to avoid predators and keep their chicks safe, they are much more likely to raise a successful brood. Go somewhere new that they don't know and they run the risk of discovering it's not suitable, wasting time and energy trying to find another nest site that hasn't already been taken. Familiarity, if you are a swallow, is key.'

My swallow skims low over the field, swift and straight as a dart, then rises, soaring over the roof of the barn. His barn. With his nest in it. He's come home.

Letters and Rings

When I arrive, writer Damian Le Bas is making Joey Grey. 'Every family has their own recipe for this, but this is the way my family do it.' It's a stew of onions, tomatoes, mushrooms and potatoes with a bit of bacon; it smells delicious. The kitchen, I notice, is immaculate. He is obviously a 'clean-up-as-you-go' cook. He takes the pan off the heat, pours coffee into two mugs and we go through to the sitting room.

The house is a bungalow. Compact. Neat as a pin. Boots lined up by the door, thick patterned carpets. There's a photo in the hall of Damian on his wedding day, his wife Candis strikingly beautiful in a full-skirted red dress, long tresses of dark hair falling over her shoulders. There are photos of an older man too. Black and white, with the grainy quality of old film. And in every photo the man is riding or standing next to a horse.

The sitting room, with its big armchairs covered in thick throws, glass-fronted cabinets full of china tea sets and 1920s fireplace with photos on the mantlepiece, is similarly immaculate.

I have the slightly odd feeling that I'm not in a home but a shrine. It's a sensation I can't quite place, but I'm almost tempted to ask if Damian actually lives here. There's no clutter – no newspapers left over from the weekend, no stray mug or wine glass on a side table – and there's something slightly unrelaxed about his demeanour, as if he feels he might be imposing on someone else's space.

We sit at the table in the window, resting our coffee mugs on the embroidered cloth. Outside, the temperature is below freezing but the sky is clear, and the sun, shining directly into the room through the net curtains, is bright and warm. We both shut our eyes for a moment to bask in its benevolent heat. I'd driven down that morning, heading east, sun in my eyes, to a suburb on the outskirts of Worthing. 'Look for the white horses' heads on the gate posts,' Damian told me. 'You won't miss the house then.'

Horses are something of a theme, inside as well as out. Along with the photographs, there is a corner cabinet on the wall behind Damian's head that is filled with china horses. 'I think I had that very one when I was a child,' I say, pointing to a prancing brown horse, front leg aloft, mane tossing.

'The horse was an emblem for my great-grandparents. It symbolised everything in life that was good for them. So that's why there are horses' heads on the end of the driveway. I think it's a bit of a traveller thing.'

Damian is a Romany. 'Well, actually I'm a "poshraht" – the Romany term for mixed blood. "Posh" is half and "raht" is blood. But I grew up mainly with my Romany relatives. I speak the language and adhere to certain customs, so I feel more genetically mixed than culturally mixed. We'll often refer to ourselves as Travellers or Gypsies, as well as Romanies, so you'll hear me use all three.'

Damian's great-grandfather is the man in the photos in the hall. They portray him as he was – a horseman. He grew up breeding and working with horses, and made his living as a rag and bone man. 'He would travel around this area with a flat cart and his horse, selling logs and taking away stuff people didn't want – recycling, I suppose you'd call it now.'

Horses were also intrinsic to his great-grandmother's childhood. She grew up on the road, the family's horse-drawn wagons travelling between farms in rural Hampshire – 'Hampshire hop country, we call it' – following a route that her ancestors had travelled since the eighteenth century. They carried knives and billhooks to do ditching and hedging, cleared stones from fields and picked potatoes. The route was dictated by the farms they worked on and both work and route were passed down the generations: lineages of farmers employing lineages of Romanies and letting them stop on their land – a relationship that stretched back centuries. It was, says Damian, a bit of a golden age for Romany people then. They had a role, a place in society that everyone understood and appreciated. But the work was backbreaking and life on the road not the carefree existence often imagined. 'The Gypsy life people romanticise is the summer Gypsy life, but there is nothing romantic about living in a wagon in the winter. It wasn't so much the rain – they could keep rain out of the camp. Their real enemy was the wind. That could destroy everything.'

In 1948, his great-grandmother's family headed south to the Worthing area, travelling with a flat cart pulled by a horse called Titch – 'Presumably 17 hands high with hooves the size of dinner plates?' I ask. 'Probably!' Damian smiles – and settled here. It is where she met her husband, whose family had been here for two generations, had bought some land and had built a house. Damian's great-grandmother was 20 years old and had never lived in a house before.

I ask if it is a sell-out to live in a house. 'Not exactly. In some ways it is seen as an enviable thing, but it is also seen as something that will change you, that you will inevitably lose some of the customs that are intrinsically linked to being on the road,' Damian says. 'But the majority of Romany people – including many of those living in Turkey, the Balkans and Eastern Europe – haven't been nomadic for centuries. Romany culture here has been fragmented, families are getting smaller, things are changing and, yes, there's a sprinkling of regret and nostalgia, but living in a house doesn't make us any less Gypsies. I'm not a nomadic Gypsy. I was born pretty settled. But my family never stopped travelling until they wanted to. It was when they got a bit of land where they could settle that they were happy to stop.' Land, he explains, is more highly prized than a house. There is room for the extended family to park their trailers and to keep the old ways going. An open fire is the heart of any gathering and is a particularly important way of mourning someone's death, when sometimes hundreds of people will gather around a fire. 'You can't really do that in a flat or a terraced house.'

Damian's maternal grandfather bought a piece of land on the edge of Worthing in 1976. He built a house there and stables for the horses he bought and sold. There was a breaker's yard for sorting scrap, the family's flower business and trailers and chalets so the whole family could be there. He called it *Savi Maski Granza*. The Barn of Laughter. Damian's parents were both artists. They lived there too, in a trailer, although moved to a council house when Damian was four years old. 'But it can take travellers who settle a while to make up their minds,' Damian laughs, so they stayed just as often in a trailer on his grandfather's land. And his home was not so much a place but his extended family, moving between houses and trailers. 'I think family is home for many people,' he says, 'but it certainly is for travellers.' And it was a transitional time. Many of the older generation of his family had grown up in wagons and tents, they still had the connection to the old ways, to the remnants of a partly mobile way of life. They were tough, he remembers, physically able to put up with anything, but also really kind-hearted and provided a visceral connection to his heritage.

Damian describes living at his grandfather's place as chaos – happy chaos, but he wouldn't invite his school friends there because he knew it was manifestly different from the way any of them lived, and even among the teachers at his primary school, he was aware of the discrimination that follows Romanies wherever they go. His grandfather's place was his refuge from all that. There, he was just like everyone else, treated like everyone else. He worked, helping his great-grandmother on her flower stall and selling Christmas trees in the winter, even when he was as young as 11. And as he got older, in his mid-teens, he travelled with the men doing roofing and building jobs, labouring for them.

But he had a parallel life. Damian, despite the unkindness of some of his teachers and fellow pupils, excelled at school. He would come back and recite the names of dinosaurs to his uncle Job, who would be astounded and delighted that one of their offspring had learned all those long, complicated words. The family was proud of him but many of them were deeply uneasy when the chance arose for Damian to go to Christ's Hospital, a very traditional private boarding school founded in the sixteenth century. It has a bursary programme, offering places to academically able children whose families are not wealthy enough to pay the fees.

In traveller culture, Damian tells me, even when you are as young as 10 or 11, although not considered an adult, you are still old enough to be allowed some agency. His parents discussed it with him, giving him the choice, knowing that it was a decision that could change the course of his life. And Damian thinks, in part, that's what his mother wanted for him. Romany herself, she knew the realities of the future that was already mapped out for Damian. 'Travellers never ask where you're from because it is a question they hate to be asked themselves. Some will consider it not only stupid, but offensive. They ask, instead, "Whose you one of then?" They want to know what your family is called because family reputation tells them all they need to know.' Damian's family had a reputation for being hard – 'Roguish, shall we say' – and his mother worried her intellectual child would suffer saddled with that reputation; she wanted him to have the option to follow a different path.

He agreed to take the exam, not believing for a moment that he would pass it. His marks were good. He was offered a place and, at the age of 11, he left everything he knew to enter what he describes as 'a mad world to me. I don't think the school had changed significantly since it was built. It was all parquet and stone floors – no carpet – and I just remember how cold that floor was. There were stuffed animal heads everywhere, rugby, Latin slang, weird customs . . .' And he felt, he said, completely destroyed by homesickness: 'They call it homesickness, but that was undercooking it.'

Interestingly, there is no Romany word, Damian tells me, to describe what he was feeling, no equivalent of the Welsh *hiraeth* that represents a feeling of longing for home that is akin to the fathomless grief of loss. I wonder, after I leave and I'm mulling over our conversation, whether it is because there is no need for such a word in Romany culture, as although their ties to a particular place may go back generations, home for them, Damian had said, was more of an internal thing, wrapped up in familiar voices and language. The Romany way was always to live together, their homes built on the bonds of the extended family, and that was something they never left.

Damian's father and grandfather were both dead against him

going away to school and as soon as they heard how much he was missing home, called for him to get out and come back. Had he run away, he said, he would have run back to the Barn of Laughter, to the happy chaos of his grandfather's place. But his great-grandmother, although also ambivalent about him going away to school, had a strong belief in education. She had taught herself to read and write, and when Damian decided to stick it out and stay at school, she wrote to him every week. In those letters were the voices and the language of his people. They were his link to home. He overcame his homesickness, lived up to his academic promise and won a scholarship to Oxford. He wore his father's buckle ring, took the letters from his great-grandmother and, leaving behind the rigid regime of his boarding school, navigated a new way of life, creating a routine for himself, working under his own steam.

Some of his mother's family had settled near Oxford and occasionally he would visit. 'They would cook me traditional travellers' food like Joey Grey and rasher pudding, stuff like that.' Rasher pudding, he explains, is like a savoury jam roly-poly, using bacon and onions in place of the jam. It was, he says, a way of making a small amount of meat go a lot further and was a staple for the field workers. And he smoked. There were always a lot of smokers at the big gatherings around the fire at his grandfather's place. 'I think I had my first fag when I was about ten, which isn't good is it?! I was never a smoker's smoker. Never enjoyed it like some people enjoy it, but it wasn't about the nicotine. It was having the embers and the smoke around me: a miniature fire that reminded me of home.'

He emerged, three years later, with a first-class degree but no real sense of where that led him. 'I'd had some experience selling flowers. I'd done a bit of labouring, but I was more of an academic than anything else.' The logical next step, he assumed, was to return to Oxford to do a postgrad but, bewilderingly, his tutors weren't encouraging. Feeling angry and betrayed he headed to London, and tried to find his niche. He got work on a fashion magazine, in a pub, in a PR firm, a marketing company. He headed back to Worthing to see his family one weekend 'and it all just kind of collapsed in on me. I sort of lost my mind, spent a month in bed.' It was his mother's idea to take him to a hypnotherapist. 'He told me I had a suppressed desire to be a writer and if I didn't address it, I was going to be ill.'

Damian worked in journalism for eight years before approaching a literary agent. It was only when he was asked by the agent what he would write about that a realisation struck him: living on the road, as his great-grandmother had, as other members of his family had, gave them something he didn't have. 'There was something in them, an ability to survive but also to live in the moment and really appreciate the simple things in life, like light and heat and water, in a way that I couldn't. And I was jealous of that.' So he told the literary agent he'd been thinking about travelling around all the old Gypsy stopping places, sleeping in his van and experiencing a side of his heritage he had never explored before. 'It was also in some ways to settle a score between me and my own people, the ones who would say, "Well, you've never lived on the road . . ." So, I thought, "Right. I will."'

In 2015, he set forth in a transit van. It was very much *not* a camper van. The inside was lined with plywood but there was no heating, no cooking facilities. Damian was unfazed. He'd lived in trailers without heating before and cooking in the same space you sleep is considered *mokkadi* – against Romany hygiene rules – so he planned to live on ready-made food or eat out. He put a rug on the floor and installed a camp bed. His great-grandmother gave him a rose-covered bed spread. His grandfather, a straw hat. He hung up a couple of shirts in case he needed smart clothes at any point. He took a spare pair of shoes, his computer and SLR camera, and that was it. Just a place to sleep and change his clothes. 'I had no stove, no means to make tea or anything.'

He shows me a photograph. It was spartan, its order almost military. Functional and cheerless, despite the rose-covered bed spread. He scrolls to find another photo. 'This is what it looked like a year later. One thing I learned about living on the road is that when it's cold and wet and you're living in a really spartan environment, it is as miserable as sin. If you've got nice things to look at – bright colours, pictures of your family – it makes it seem a whole lot easier. That's what taught me why travellers were so obsessed with decoration; why the old wagons were gilded and painted and carved the way they were. It made a tough life more bearable.' The space I look at now is unrecognisable. There are curtains and drapes around the sides of the van, another rug, lots of big, patterned cushions with fringing at their edges and richly decorated throws. There's a mirror, a Romany lantern, a painting by his mother and family photographs. A small statue of

St Sara-la-Kâli, patron saint of the Roma. A lamp, a folding chair, a radio. And he now has a stainless steel water jack, a generator and a stove. There's an enamel kettle, pots and pans. He'd given the van a name – *Kushti Bok* – Romany for 'good luck'. He'd made himself a home. And emotionally that is what it had become.

When he drove to another new place, all he had to do was go into the back of the van and he would be surrounded by the safe and the familiar. 'I would unpack all my stuff, put pictures of my family all around, light a candle, burn some incense. The fact that it was small made it special. I knew where everything was. I was a bit militant about order and cleanliness, but you have to be when you're living in a small space. I felt almost like I was transporting a magical chamber with me. It made me feel that tug of home. I miss it still, as you can probably tell.'

There's a map at the beginning of the book Damian wrote: a map of Gypsy Britain. It charts the places he went, first following the route between the stopping places his great-grandmother's ancestors followed for hundreds of years. Then moving on to other parts of the country, to the stopping places of other families. 'We've been here a long time and these places mean a lot to us. There are so many people who think Gypsies don't belong anywhere, but that's ridiculous. We're just as tethered to these places as anyone else. Perhaps more so. Gypsies were only nomadic until they could find somewhere to stop, ideally for as long as possible.'

'What made you stop?' I ask.

'I didn't want to do another winter. I'd tasted it and I didn't like the taste. But also, I'd come to the end of the particular journey I was on. I didn't fetishise travelling anymore. I was content.'

Together with his wife, he moved back to the Barn of Laughter, to a trailer on his grandfather's land. This house, the house I've come to, was his great-grandmother's home. After she and her family moved to the Worthing area, she met her husband and for the first time in her life, lived not in a wagon, but a house. They moved around a bit, always in the same area, but this house was their last home. They bought it in 1996 and Damian spent much of his childhood here. 'I used to stay here all the time and I always felt welcome here in a way I rarely felt welcome anywhere else.'

After her husband died, his great-grandmother continued to live here, until, at the age of 95, she died. She was one of the most pivotal people in Damian's life. Her letters to him when he was away at school, and that he keeps to this day, were the tangible link to the home he missed so much. She was always his champion, but more, she was his constant, anchoring him to his heritage, to his history, to his family. To where he belongs.

'The thing is,' he says, unconsciously twisting the ring on his finger, a miniature replica of a Western saddle in finely tooled gold given to him by his grandfather a couple of years before he died, 'travellers are very funny about somebody's physical possessions after they've died. They believe their spirit lingers on in them. In the old days, when someone died, their wagon would be burned. All their china would be smashed up. Horses had to be sold to another family who lived far enough away that you would never see them again. Even now, it is a massive taboo to drive a dead person's motor. We have to burn all the clothes my great-grandmother wore. When a woman dies, it is another woman of the family who has to sort the clothes for burning, so my mother is doing that. I'm supposed to get rid of her cooking stuff but it's perfectly alright. It's a waste. So I'm trying to negotiate with my feelings, trying to find a way to navigate between the emotional – and environmental – impact of chucking everything away and the traveller in me that says it's all got to go. My great-grandmother was one of the last ones that had those ways, so we'll honour that and do what she would have done. There is a side of me that wants to do everything the old-fashioned way, but sometimes I feel like I can't, that I haven't got the strength, or maybe it'll have to wait. I don't know, to be honest.'

But then there's the house. In Gypsy culture, material heirlooms, like the ring Damian wears, can be handed down to other members of the family, but only when the person giving them away is still alive. When they die, the family is only meant to hold onto their legacy of ancestry: language, skills, memories, knowledge of the family history. Those are the things that hold greater importance to Gypsies, more so than material goods. Damian's great-grandmother was acutely aware of this, knew the unease the family would feel about Damian taking on her house when she died, so on numerous occasions she tried to tell him it was his. 'She'd drop massive hints that I would try and ignore. When she was really sick, she said, "You're the captain of the ship now, mate," in front of everyone. It was a declaration. Her way of saying, "I'm doing this now, so you don't have to get rid of the place."'

He moved in a couple of months ago but admits it is strange being here. 'The people who made this place aren't here anymore, and the fact that she has left it to me hasn't gone down brilliantly with everybody. I don't think anyone else in my family would have kept it. I think they'd have all have sold it and I thought about doing that, but for some reason I couldn't bring myself to do it, not yet anyway.'

So he's still edging his way in. 'It's a managed transition.' He doesn't want to do what most people would: take out everything valuable and gut it. He's put some of his own photographs on the wall; there's a photo of his wife's great-grandmother sitting on the steps of her wagon in Kent, a throw given to his wife by her father on the sofa. He wants to get the chimney swept so the fire can be lit, but for the moment, he burns sage and lights a candle in the grate. And his van is here, his home for almost two years, parked at the back.

'I love being here. It's where I wrote most of my book. She believed in what I was trying to do and the only review I really cared about when the book was finished was hers. She loved it.' And he's writing again. It's a good place to be for that. He's getting a lot done. He's silent for a bit, looking out of the window. ' "Treat this place as your home, mate," she told me, thousands of times. More than a thousand times. So, you know, I've been given permission, haven't I, to stay?'

Oh, give me land, lots of land under starry skies above,
Don't fence me in.
Let me ride through the wide open country that I love,
Don't fence me in.
Let me be by myself in the evenin' breeze,
And listen to the murmur of the cottonwood trees,
Send me off forever but I ask you please,
Don't fence me in.

From 'Don't Fence Me In', words and music by Cole Porter

Seeing Green

———

Alice and I are walking through the woods between our two houses. It's late spring and the beech trees are in leaf, a fluttering canopy of vibrant green above our heads. Spring sunshine finds its way between the leaves, creating a kaleidoscope pattern of light and shade beneath our feet. And the bluebells are out, which is why we've chosen to walk this particular route. We've walked it at this time of year many times and the enchantment never fades. There's a spot where the ground slopes away towards the unseen river below where the bluebells are so profuse that they form an unbroken carpet of colour so intense it seems to radiate from the flowers and hang in a low, shimmering mist of soft, hazy blue above them.

Alice needs this walk, needs the calming, therapeutic effect that putting one foot in front of the other has on her troubled head. It frees her thoughts and worries so she can begin to articulate them in fits and starts. It's her work.

I've known Alice for almost a decade. She's a grafter, a

perfectionist, one of those people who has a niggling voice in her head that never stops her questioning whether she is doing enough, well enough. Her job is demanding mentally and physically, the hours long, but she's used to all that. Alice is a vet. What's troubling her is that so many of the people she is working with are unhappy. Vets and veterinary nurses are leaving in droves and the suicide rate is shockingly high – four times the national average. Alice has lost friends and colleagues. Everyone, she tells me, seems to have lost someone. The veterinary world has become corporate – the emphasis now is on satisfying shareholders, rather than clients or patients. No one is listening to the desperate needs of staff, and without staff, client and patient needs are not met. The profession is on its knees. Alice is on her knees.

I mull our conversation over for a pace or two, then stop. 'You could just leave,' I say. 'Set up again on your own.' I'm playing devil's advocate here, but only in part. Alice is extremely good at her job, has years of experience and is very well-liked and respected. I have few, if any, doubts that she would get all the support and encouragement she would need to make her own business a success. She looks back at me, eyes darting, as thoughts race through her head. I know how much this idea will appeal to her. I also know the fears that will, at this moment, be crowding her brain. She crumples. Leans against a tree, needing the comforting solidity of its trunk to stop her collapsing entirely. Her face is stricken, her voice panicked. 'I can't,' she says. 'I can't leave and risk losing my home.'

Alice studied psychology at university, got a first-class degree and went straight on to do a masters in clinical psychology. In her early twenties, she was working in the NHS, in adult mental health and child and family services. 'I was very young and idealistic. I worried constantly that I wasn't making enough of a difference to the people I was treating. I was working in this enormous system and seeing people with such profound problems – child sexual abuse, victims of abuse now struggling as adults. We would have eight sessions and that was supposed to fix them.'

She was living in a shared house with 'a lot of bitchy girls'. It was a miserable place to come back to, particularly after long and challenging days at work, and she was desperate for her own place and her own space. She'd become friends with Ian – an engineering student who made her laugh – at university. They started going out and their relationship continued after they left. 'Why don't we move in together?' he suggested. 'You're miserable.'

Ian, Alice laughs, was not a natural homemaker. At university, he made no attempt to personalise his room, make it feel homely or even comfortable. 'He just kept all his stuff – bits of crockery, his rugby kit – all jumbled up and often unwashed in a cardboard box at the bottom of his bed. He had a single poster of Boris Karloff's Frankenstein stuck up, wonkily, with masking tape and he lived on Doll noodles.' Alice, by contrast, had perfected the art of making anywhere she lived feel as beautiful and welcoming as possible – 'Even the soulless, boxy room I had in the 1970s Wimpey Home we lived in when we were kids.'

'Come on then,' she said to Ian. 'Let's do it. Let's buy a house and I'll make us a fabulous home!'

They bought a little house in Godalming, not far from the university, but in time, they both began to feel hemmed in and yearned for a bit of green space around them. 'Green is very important to me,' Alice says, and I absolutely recognise that sentiment. I too remember the oppressiveness of city life, the feeling of always being surrounded, that everywhere you looked there were buildings and roads and cars and people. Of yearning, in the very core of my being, for a clear, uninterrupted view. To be able to look out over a wide green space to the horizon and the sky.

She and Ian moved to a county Alice's dad had always loved and would bring his family to for camping holidays. The house they found was in a village. It was a tiny, ugly building, but they didn't care. It was on top of a hill and it looked out over a rolling patchwork of green fields, so they loved it. And it was perhaps this rural setting that made Alice think back to the books she'd read over and over again as a child: the stories of James Herriot. 'I loved those books. I loved the part he played in the community and the relationships he had with the people. And of course, it made me want to be a vet.' But she hadn't applied to study veterinary medicine because she didn't think she'd get the grades she needed. But now she had a first-class degree and a masters. She applied to vet school and was accepted.

They moved house, not to be closer to Alice's university, but because they started to feel scrutinised and policed in the village. People complained because they had chickens. Someone reported them to the parish council because they hadn't trimmed their hedge. 'It wasn't home anymore. Home, I realised, needed to be somewhere you could be unashamedly yourself, where you could tuck yourself away, relax and rejuvenate. Somewhere quiet.' They found a cottage on the Herefordshire border with Wales. It was a 'doer-upper', a very traditional, tiny stone cottage, built directly onto the earth and surrounded by woodland, with all the potential, they believed, to be exactly what they wanted. Ian worked on the cottage every night after work and Alice came home from vet school at weekends to help him. Although its size meant there wasn't a lot of scope to do much, she did what she always does – 'Ian built the walls and I made it into a cosy nest: warm and comfortable and beautiful. It was our little retreat in the woods and we loved it.'

Alice qualified as a vet and finally they could move into the cottage together. She was offered a job. 'It was a really traditional, community mixed practice, looking after farm animals and pets. There are not many of those around anymore. I was delighted. It was the Herriot life that had inspired me to spend all those years re-training. But then, six months after I started the job, I got pregnant.' This was an unexpected joy for Alice. She'd suffered an ectopic pregnancy while taking her university finals and had been dangerously ill. Doctors told her it was likely she would have problems conceiving again so she and Ian had more or less resigned themselves to being unable to have children.

When she told the partners at the practice that she was expecting a baby, they were furious. 'They accused me of being deceitful and said they would never trust me again. Then they just didn't speak to me. I tried to tell them that although I was absolutely delighted that I was pregnant against all the odds, I hadn't worked as hard as I had to get my vet's qualification to sit at home with a baby for ten years. That I understood the short-term inconvenience for them but I absolutely intended to come back after the baby was born and Ian was more than prepared to share half of our parenting duties. They weren't having any of it.'

The months at work leading up to the birth of her son Josh were awful. She was sidelined, frozen out, given no support. When Josh was three months old, before her maternity leave was over, she offered to do odd days for them to help, but they refused. They said she wasn't welcome until she could come back full time. 'I was heartbroken. I didn't know what to do. I just thought they were never going to forgive me and my working life would be impossible. We didn't want to leave the area we had grown to love and my parents had moved here to be close to us. I couldn't find another job within a realistic distance and so the only option I could think of was to set up on my own. Ian agreed we should give it a go.'

They formulated a plan over the following year. Alice would be the sole vet in the practice, which would require her to do all the out-of-hours on-call work too. For that to be possible, they would have to combine work with home and live in the same building as the practice. 'It seemed a perfect solution and I really believed it would be fine. I'd basically be working from home; I could look after Josh and still work all the hours I had to.'

In hindsight, she wonders why they decided to shake up their lives in such a dramatic fashion. Having Josh had enhanced her love for their little woodland cottage even more. They'd created a nursery for him, stencilled hares on the walls – 'I have a thing about hares . . .' – and she would sit feeding him in his little room, listening to the radio, completely content. But they sold it and bought a Georgian house in a nearby town, big enough to turn the ground floor into Alice's veterinary practice and for them all to live on the floor above. They took out a Treasury loan to buy the house and fit out the ground floor and in just eight weeks the practice was open. 'I was so confident it was going to be a fabulous community practice, one that would be as caring and compassionate to owners as well as their animals. But neither Ian nor I had any business experience. We were incredibly naïve.'

Initially, Ian continued his work as an engineer, Alice ran the practice and they would do the admin and the books together in the evenings. They had put in a kitchen upstairs but the rest of their living space remained a building site. They had no time or money for Alice to create a cosy nest. There were simply not enough hours for her to see patients during the day, be on call at night, manage the business and look after her child. She had been overambitious and unrealistic, and it was beginning to take its toll.

Ian, who wasn't really enjoying his job, gave it up to be the practice's business manager. But losing his salary only added to the pressure. There was no escape, no retreat, no cosy nest. Home and work had become one. They never left the building. They became completely overwhelmed. 'I was so desperate to have somewhere I could go to just rejuvenate,' Alice says, 'but there simply wasn't time and there wasn't anywhere to go.' Not only that, they were financially trapped. 'I was working harder and harder and getting more and more depleted and still we had no money. My relationship with Ian was beginning to suffer. He blamed me for getting us into the mess we were in. Said it was my idea, so it was my responsibility to get us out of it. We were having huge, vicious, damaging arguments in the dead of night when Josh was asleep, and I was getting to the point when I just couldn't do it anymore.'

The final straw for Alice came when Ian's behaviour began to affect other people. 'While he was just angry with me, I found it difficult to distinguish where my culpability stopped and his began. When he became unreasonable and intolerant with others like Josh, I suddenly saw this couldn't go on. We were all suffering. We were all chronically unhappy.'

She left as a temporary measure and moved into a friend's house behind the practice where Josh could come and go between the two houses. Respite came from an old school friend who she hadn't seen for 35 years. Tony was now living in New Zealand and they had been in touch only sporadically, but now he messaged her and said, 'Come out here and have a break.'

Tony's life had also been in turmoil. His marriage had broken down and he was trying to sell his business. He and Alice spent two weeks together walking the trails that wind through the back country of New Zealand. When he had to return to work, Alice continued travelling on her own in a camper van for six weeks. 'I walked and walked and then sometimes I'd just sit. It was exactly what I needed to get my head straight again.'

Ian met her at the airport on her return, hopeful that after her time away they could repair their damaged relationship and get back together. Meeting him there was excruciating. 'My heart broke for him – for us all really – but I just couldn't go back. Too much had happened.' But she promised to find a solution to sorting out their business. She made an appointment with the bank, spent many hours putting together a financial plan to present to them and arranged to meet them at the practice. She arrived early to find her practice and former home surrounded by police. She was arrested on the spot and detained while officers searched the premises.

Alice was signed off work with severe stress and sleep disturbance while she fought to clear her name. All charges against her were dropped but it gradually became apparent what had happened. A close friend had invited Ian to be part of a scheme to help him out of his and Alice's dire financial situation. The scheme, though, was fraudulent. Ian's friend was found guilty of multiple offences and both he and Ian were sent to prison.

Alice was broken. Their entire life savings had gone into buying the building and creating the practice. Ian declared himself bankrupt and all their debts were transferred solely to Alice. She couldn't repay them. She lost her business. She lost her home. She lost her car. She had to re-home her dogs. She and Josh, now ten years old, had to move in with her parents, who were deeply upset, angry and shocked by what had happened. Alice and Josh holed up in the little room they were sharing, watching *Friends* videos every night, while Alice sunk deeper and deeper into depression. It was Tony, once again, who offered a way out. 'I've managed to sell my business and I've bought a boat. Why don't you just come? It will cost you no money. You and Josh can sit next to me on the boat somewhere beautiful and quiet. You don't have to bring anything. Just come.'

Before she and Josh left the UK, Alice shipped four brightly coloured cushion covers she had salvaged from her few remaining possessions. With them, she packed a small bronze hare she'd bought a few years before, a photograph of their dog and a montage of photographs for Josh of all the important people in his life. 'I'm like a little magpie. Having things that are beautiful to me has always been the way I've made somewhere feel like home. And I love colour. It does something to my brain. Makes it peaceful. Even though I knew we wouldn't be on the boat forever, I really needed for it to feel like a home, and I knew all it would take was four cushions and a hare.'

They lived on Tony's boat for ten months, travelling from island to island in the Pacific before ending up back in New Zealand. And the boat really did feel like home, almost instantly. It was, she says, the best thing she has ever done, and she would have stayed, would happily have made the boat her permanent home. But she knew when it was the right time for Josh to come back to the UK. He needed to be with his friends again. To be back at school. And to see his father.

They rented a little house back in the same town they'd lived in before they went to New Zealand. The previous tenants had left it in a poor state, and it was damp and dirty, but she didn't care. She knew she could make it a home for her and Josh. She had some things in storage, such as a couple of IKEA bookshelves that she had bought when she and Ian first moved to Herefordshire, and her much-treasured stuffed owls – roadkill that she had picked up because they were so beautiful. She'd found a taxidermist who could stuff them and mount them in glass cases. Her tawny owl and barn owl were given pride of place on the bookshelves, along with her James Herriot books and her childhood copies of *Watership Down* and *The L-Shaped Room*. There were a couple of small ceramics, some things Josh had made, her hares and her paintings. Her favourite, a vibrant landscape by the artist Lynda Jones, she put by her bed so she could look at green while she fell asleep. She got a job as a vet again. Josh returned to school.

The one thing that was missing was Tony. Their friendship had become a relationship, though he had been so profoundly hurt and upset when she left the boat to return to the UK that he didn't contact her for months. Then one day he messaged out of the blue – just a text. 'Can I come back?' He set sail from New Zealand and she met him half way in South Africa. It was Christmas. Her present to him was a key to her little rented house.

They lived there for four years until the house, already dilapidated when Alice moved in, became overwhelmed by damp. The carpets were being eaten by moths; the front door wouldn't lock and even Alice's beautiful things couldn't make it feel like the cosy nest. The restorative place of retreat. And after years of turbulence, she keenly missed having a home that she owned. That was truly hers.

She and Tony found a new-build house. It sits tucked in a steep-sided valley and although it has other houses around it, it still feels very private. Still feels like a retreat. A stream runs through the garden and it looks out over trees and green, the view and the colour that makes Alice happiest. Her bookshelves are up in the living room and her owls are there, with her beloved books and her hares. The cushions she shipped to the other side of the world are on the sofa; her favourite painting is on the wall. Tony's parents gave them some money as a house-warming present and she bought a rug, a patchwork of colours that are set off perfectly by the wooden floor and complimented by the house plants that have become her newfound passion. Tony and Josh had little influence on what went where. They left Alice to it, knowing it is her thing, the thing she loves most. Making a home. But she is scared. Buying this house has been a financial stretch for both of them. She knows what it is like to lose a home. She can't let it happen again.

We stand in the woods and hug. 'Let's see if there might be another way,' I say.

The First House

———

I lived in the house in Shepherd's Bush with my husband Ludo for seven years. It was the only place since leaving my childhood home that I had lived in for so long. The intervening years had been spent, fairly typically, living the transient existence of the young and unburdened, cadging places to stay for a week or two before graduating to renting rooms in shared houses. I'd had a short stint in a squat, bunking down on the floor of the sitting room, using the sofa cushions as a mattress. And I'd spent a year in Africa, travelling alone, unfettered, eking out my hard-earned savings and going in whatever direction chance pointed me. I stayed in houses, hostels, in the back of someone's lorry. I slept in tents, shacks and, one memorable night, rolled up in a blanket on top of a wall. So, the cottage in Shepherd's Bush, built to house workers on the new railways of the Victorian era, was a first in many ways. It was the first place that either Ludo or I had ever bought; the first place we lived in together; the first place in our adult lives that we could do whatever we liked – within the confines of our bank balance – because it was ours.

I remember going to see it for the first time, following the estate agent in his shiny suit and shoes up through the narrow gate that led off the pavement, along a short concrete path with a shaggy patch of lawn beside it, to the front door. Two floors, red brick and narrow, it shared its side walls with the identical cottages on either side. A couple of steps through the door took you to the foot of the staircase, up which was a tiny, old-fashioned bathroom with a plastic bath and cracked lino floor. There were two bedrooms, one whose window overlooked the line of terraced cottages behind, and one at the front, with windows overlooking the road. Next to it was a box room, not big enough for a bed, but with a window and enough room for a small desk and bookshelves. Downstairs, the front room had a fireplace, with ornate dark green tiles either side of a small grate, a wooden surround and a mantelpiece. The room at the back had a door into the concrete yard where the former privy had been turned into a storage shed. The kitchen was tucked in the corner beneath the angle of the stairs. The house was being sold for £89,000. With our wedding present deposit money and the mortgage we were offered – remarkably, given that neither of us had 'proper' permanent jobs and our earnings were laughable – we could afford it. We moved in without the need for a removal van. All we owned could be packed in a Renault 5 and a Fiat Uno.

It was a thrill. We were the archetypal newly-weds, spending every evening and weekend up ladders covered in paint, stripping floorboards with those machines that cover everything, and every part of you, in a choking cloak of dust. We trawled second-hand shops and hired vans to transport bits of furniture given to us by our families. We had my granny's chintz-covered sofa and a large dark wardrobe from the house of Ludo's grandmother. We bought an Ikea kitchen and installed it ourselves, managing not to kill each other in the process. We bought plants for the tiny yard at the back, including a clematis to climb around the front door. I longed for a dog but we got a pet rat instead. It was home. Our home. And we loved it. But it didn't stop me feeling restless.

Two years after we were married, we rented out our beloved little house to a friend to cover the mortgage payments and flew to South Africa. It was 1994; South Africa had a new president. Change that no one had ever imagined possible had come about. The news brought excitement, a crackle of energy, the frisson of the unknown. We had to be part of it. We rented a tiny house in a Cape Town suburb. It was entirely empty: no fridge, no cooker, no furniture. And we bought an old, not entirely reliable, Ford Cortina pick-up. We used it to go and buy a mattress-sized piece of foam rubber, a Calor Gas camping stove, a cool box, a couple of saucepans, a set of cutlery with red plastic handles, a few plates and bowls and some rudimentary bits of kitchen equipment. And moved in. We lived there for a couple of months, until reality hit. Our tentative dream of moving to South Africa long-term had been shattered when our application to emigrate was turned down the morning before we got on the plane. Undaunted – we had to be, our friend had already moved into our house – we still hoped to be able to work and to stay as long as possible. But that didn't turn out to be as straightforward as we had hoped either.

It was Ludo who eventually pointed out that there wasn't anything very adventurous about sitting in an empty house watching our savings disappear into the landlord's pocket. If we could only be here for a short time, we needed to make the most of it. So, we gave up the house, put the mattress in the back of the pick-up, packed up everything else into cardboard boxes and put those in the pick-up too. Home was now a white Ford Cortina with a yellow go-faster stripe and the open road.

We lived in – or perhaps more accurately, out of – that pick-up for around four months. We travelled thousands of miles, driving north from Cape Town to the border with Namibia, on to Zimbabwe, post-war Mozambique, Swaziland and back into South Africa, returning to Cape Town from the east. I loved that time, that way of life. The simple self-sufficiency of it. Although we didn't have a plan as such – no fixed route with goals that had to be reached and no time limit – it never felt like aimless wandering. Nor did we ever feel rootless. The van absolutely became home. It was our fixed point, our anchor. Our kitchen was in one cardboard box; tent, roll mats and sleeping bags in another. We had a bucket, jerry cans for water, firewood, a metal grill for cooking over a fire and a cast iron pot with three stout legs that remains the best piece of cooking equipment I have ever owned. Oh, and 'magic string' – a parting gift from Ludo's mother before we left England. It was a ball of entirely normal string but, she told us, a ball of string can provide the solution to many a conundrum. Which makes it magic. And so it proved: replacing broken guy ropes, hanging mosquito nets, providing a temporary bootlace. Tied to the wing mirror of the pick-up and stretched around the trunk of a nearby tree, it was the perfect washing line.

We broke down at least once in every country we drove through, but the joy of being off the beaten track in a continent like Africa is that the people you come across, even if you have to wait a while or walk a distance to meet them, tend to be endlessly resourceful and unfazed by the apparent terminal condition of our pick-up. With often the most basic of tools, occasional muttered curses and, once in a while, a bit of brute force, it would be cajoled into life again and off we'd go.

We had just crossed the border from Mozambique into Swaziland and had promised ourselves a night in a campsite. After almost a month of living 'wild', our standards of personal hygiene had slipped somewhat and we, and our clothes, were in need of a proper wash. Thirty miles over the border, coasting down a long, straight, empty road, red earth and scrubby bush stretching away to the horizon on either side, the pick-up juddered and coughed and slid to a stubborn, unrelenting halt.

We stayed in the compound of a family who lived just off the road for three days, sleeping in the round, mud-walled hut, thatched with twigs and grass, that the family reserved for guests. It stood slightly apart from the other huts, grouped around a carefully swept area of hard-packed earth, shaded by large trees. While their neighbour, Thomas, who knew something about cars, and Ludo tried to coax the pick-up back to life, I spent the days with the women of the family, helping them with their chores. We walked to the river to collect water, hoed the soil between neatly planted rows of vegetables to clear the weeds, picked unfamiliar leaves and pulled up strange tubers to cook for the evening meal.

The girls all went to school and spoke excellent English, and were as curious about my life as I was about theirs. They asked me to describe our house, were wide-eyed to discover that running water, electricity and indoor bathrooms were not luxuries but just normal. 'And your garden?' they asked. 'Where is your mealie patch?' Mealie is the local word for maize, a staple in many parts of Africa where it is often ground into a course flour and turned into a porridge or stiff paste. Every household, even those in towns and cities, had a mealie patch. When we had been passing through Harare, in Zimbabwe, we had been invited to the house of a man we met while, once again, getting the car fixed. The brother of the garage owner, our host, was one of the rising number of middle-class, Black Zimbabweans. He worked in a bank and lived with his wife and family in a neat, painted brick house in the suburbs. Growing on the small piece of ground right in front of his house was a healthy thicket of maize plants, taller than me, thick, ripening cobs peering between the heavy droop of the leaves. A home is not a home without a mealie patch. The girls were aghast when I told them we didn't have one, that neither the concrete yard at the back of our house nor the patch of grass at the front were big enough nor suitable for cultivating mealies. They went into an instant huddle then announced that we must live with them. They seized my all-too willing hand and led me to the place on their land where they said we could build a hut. 'We'll help you!' they chorused. 'And your mealie patch will be there!' and they pointed together to a flat area of sparsely vegetated soil, just waiting, it seemed to me, for someone to plant it.

The memories of that place: the girls clinging to my hands and arms, excitedly making plans for me. The smell of the sun-baked earth. The bright, clean light. The space. The space that seemed infinite. No buildings. No roads. Just land and sky and me. Those memories would crowd my head when our savings ran out and we returned to our house in Shepherd's Bush, when I felt sad and lost and unable to fit back into the life we'd lived so happily before. I had the sensation of not being entirely present, that some part of me had dawdled as we made our way back and failed to catch up. And now the home that we had painted and furnished with such love and pride, the home where we spent our first married Christmas eating smoked salmon sandwiches on my granny's chintz sofa and watching *Doctor Zhivago*, where we'd gathered around the table with our friends on countless nights, to eat and drink and laugh and sing, didn't feel like home anymore. And I didn't know where did.

The Homing Pigeon

The rock dove, or feral pigeon, is a bird familiar to everyone and rarely admired by anyone. They are the birds that rise up in noisily fluttering clouds from urban squares, that flock around café tables and benches where people are eating, pecking at fallen scraps. The birds that roost and nest on windowsills or ledges or in alcoves of city buildings, littering the ground beneath them with shit and feathers. Pigeons are generally regarded as vermin: disease-ridden, dirty and a nuisance.

Yet humans have relied on these birds for millennia. The Egyptians were using them in 3000 BC. The Ancient Greeks too. Genghis Khan, the twelfth-century Sultan of Syria, and Julius Caesar utilised these birds; as did news reporter Paul Reuter in the nineteenth century; French, British and American armies in the twentieth century; Indian police forces in the twenty-first century. They have carried messages, announcements and breaking news; delivered urgent medicines, secret microfilms and contraband, because these birds have an innate skill that is truly remarkable.

Pigeons can navigate their way home across huge distances with incredible accuracy. They use a number of methods, relying in part on the sun and on magnetoreception, which enables them to detect the Earth's magnetic field. But studies have also shown that they also use infrasound, smell and visual landmarks to determine their route. They fly fast too, averaging 60mph, and can cover hundreds, even thousands, of miles in one journey. In 1931, a pigeon was released in the town of Arras, in southern France, and 24 days later, it arrived in the Vietnamese capital of Saigon, having flown 7,200 miles.

Humans living thousands of years ago must have noticed the astonishing abilities of these remarkable birds and, at some point, realised that they could utilise them. But to do that, they needed to be able to control where the pigeons considered to be their home. Thus, the rock dove was the first bird ever to be domesticated, returning after a foray to the home their owners provided for them. Which presumably meant that in ancient Egypt, the equivalent of giving your phone number to someone you wanted to communicate with regularly was handing over some of your pigeons and taking some of theirs in return. Any time one of you wanted to tell something to the other, you would simply write the information on a piece of paper, attach it to the leg of one of the recipient's pigeons and let it go, trusting that its homing instinct would take it to the right place.

But pigeons used in battle to carry messages back from the

frontline had to adjust their navigational systems so they could find their way to their temporary barracks on the edge of a battlefield. During the Second World War, there were pigeon lofts in some of the strategic control centres in Britain too. The birds from these lofts would travel with troops being deployed on operations in occupied territories. Eighty-two pigeons were dropped in the Netherlands with the 1st Airborne Division Signals and each time a message needed to be sent back to HQ in London, a pigeon would fly 240 miles back across the Channel to deliver it.

These much-maligned birds have been the bearers of vital information, saved countless lives and been awarded medals for bravery, all because of their irresistible urge to return home.

Dignity and Trees

In a wide pull-in off the road, there's a green metal gate across a rutted gravel track that leads into a tall stand of gently swaying conifers. I leave my car, climb over the gate and follow the sound of a chainsaw.

The track climbs through the trees. At the crest, I spot a tall figure, gloved and helmeted, slicing timber, logs rolling away as they fall and collecting at his feet. He spots me too, shuts off the saw, the sudden silence ringing in my ears. He approaches with long strides, removing his helmet as he walks, revealing a slim, heavily bearded face and long, dark ponytail. A big, workmanlike hand shakes mine. 'I'm Mathew. Mat.'

He lives here in the woods. There is no house but as we follow the track, the conifers giving way to native broadleaf, I see a couple of wooden shelters tucked beneath the branches and, further on, a small caravan with an awning alongside, where there's a sofa, a wooden table, a couple of stools and an armchair. Work boots are stacked on a rack at the entrance beneath heavy, waterproof coats on hooks. There's an easel holding a large canvas, more paintings leaning against the wall of the caravan, flowers in a jam jar and a young woman in jeans and a jumper, a curtain of heavy blonde hair falling around her face.

'I'm Lauren, Mat's girlfriend. Hello!'

'I brought cake,' I say, handing over a loaf of lemon drizzle cake wrapped in greaseproof paper.

'Then I'll make tea,' says Lauren and disappears into the caravan.

A cat, which I am to discover goes by the superb name of Baby Bowie Don Quixote, 'or just Baby', slides out of the door as Lauren opens it, jumps up onto the sofa and gives Mat and me an imperious look.

This 15-acre patch of woodland, a mixed plantation of Douglas fir, Sitka spruce, Japanese larch and broadleaf – wild cherry, oak and sweet chestnut – belonged to Mat's father. Mat's grandfather, Claude, trained in silviculture and worked as a woodland manager in Kenya before returning to the UK and settling among the ancient trees of the Forest of Dean. He passed on his love of the woods to his son and, although Mat's father studied medicine and became a GP, his childhood connection to the forest was deep-rooted. So when he inherited some money from his aunt, the best thing to do with it, he believed, was buy trees.

Mat and his siblings grew up in an old charcoal burner's cottage on a hill above a Welsh village, a few miles from their father's woodland. Perhaps it is no coincidence that the name of the village translates as 'oak trees'. He talks of his childhood fondly. It was, he says, grounded and secure, in the house his parents still live in 44 years later, and the tree-covered hill was his playground. 'When I think back to my childhood, the words I associate with it are warmth, safety, comfort, a sense of permanence and, perhaps most of all, it was an adventure.'

It felt like a natural choice for Mat to work in forestry after school but neither his teachers nor his parents were encouraging; they didn't believe there were proper career prospects in the timber industry. They would have liked him to study law but instead he read politics and went on to do a master's in public administration. 'It would have stood me in good stead to work in local government but I just wasn't interested in doing that. I hadn't given up on the idea of working in forestry, so I laboured on building sites so I could earn the money to get my chainsaw qualifications.'

Mat went from the cosy stability of his upbringing to the insecurity of being a tenant in shared houses. He found the experience stressful, felt vulnerable being at the mercy of landlords. By the time he'd reached his late twenties, he was thinking about how he could live in a way that made him feel more independent and in control of his own destiny.

He was left a little bit of money when his grandmother died. It wasn't enough for a deposit on a house of his own but enough to buy a yurt and finish training to be a tree surgeon. He got a job felling trees for a timber merchant down in Devon, where he lived in a field in his yurt for over two years. There was a dignity, he said, in owning the structure he lived in, something he missed keenly when he was renting. And it was a beautiful way to live, until the winter came. 'Then it was brutal: cold, wet and muddy.'

The yurt finally succumbed to the damp, starting to rot and fall apart. An old friend offered Mat a job back in Wales, near where he grew up and, now in his early thirties, Mat moved back in with his parents. They were retired by this time and welcomed him back, cooking him hearty meals when he came in soaked and filthy after long days outside. But for Mat, grateful as he was, it felt like a failure that he had reached that point in his life and still wasn't able to provide himself with a home of his own. 'That's what I had aspired to growing up: independence, in a property that was mine. That, for me, was the dignified way to live.'

But it was, he realised, good to be back in Wales. He'd become increasingly aware of the latent tug of *hiraeth* – the Welsh word that has no English equivalent that quite encapsulates that niggle of missing home, the ache of longing, the emotional pull of the place your heart tells you that you belong. And he felt its influence even more strongly when he was back – 'So much so that I didn't want to go away again.' He rediscovered and appreciated with renewed vigour the landscape – his landscape – and his deep connection with it. It wasn't just knowing the names of places and what they mean, and how to get from one place to another without thinking, but the more intimate things – the things you only know when you've lived in a place long enough to have gathered and collected memories, insights and experiences stretching back over years. The sound of oak leaves unfurling in the moonlight of early spring. The sun making the hills glow red in late summer. Where to find the sweetest bilberries. The smell of leaf mulch. The whispering thud of falling acorns. The way the mist snags on the hill on damp autumn mornings and drifts up in whisps with the warmth of the rising sun.

Mat stayed in Wales for a while, but when he started getting work at events and festivals, building stages and erecting lighting rigs, his life became itinerant again. He bought an old postal van and lived in it for six years, more or less permanently on the move. On the days between events, he'd take off for the coast and surf, parking up where he could. Winters, as ever, were harder. There was less work and he became more reliant on friends giving him somewhere he could stay safely in his van. And it was that reliance on the goodwill of others that made him realise that the van, although a useful resource, couldn't be a home. And that was what he needed. That was what he was ready for.

But somehow a house didn't feel like the right thing for Mat. And as someone self-employed, doing a physical job with a high risk of injury, he was worried that he might not always be able to meet the demands of a mortgage. But more fundamental than that was the desire to find a way of living that felt authentic to him. 'I wanted to create a home environment that expressed who I am and what I believe in, that used the skills and knowledge I have. By then, I'd been working with trees for 20 years. It made more sense to me to buy a woodland than a house.'

He found three acres of woodland for sale in west Wales. Mat's father, who had never lost the love of trees he inherited from his father, went along to look at it with him. Mat liked the land, could see how he could build a little access track into it, imagine where he might erect a small, timber-framed building among the trees. But his father thought it was too expensive. 'It's a rip off!' he said. 'I have my bit of woodland. Why don't you take that on and live there?'

'I've been here six years,' Mat says, 'and I've finally realised that this has always been home. We used to come camping here when we were kids. And when I came to live here and heard the church bells ring on a Thursday night, I remembered that sound from my childhood, remembered it was always on a Thursday. And it's the sounds and smells and flavours that triggered my memory, that made me feel at home. It was those things that made me understand that despite wanting to leave after school, that despite living in all sorts of different places, home was here. This is where the *hiraeth* came back.'

He makes his apologies. He has to finish cutting the logs and deliver them to a customer. He picks up his helmet and lopes off, merging with the tall, straight trunks of the conifers.

'How long have you lived here?' I ask Lauren, as she pours us more tea.

'Coming up for two years,' she says. She's an artist – the canvases are hers – and she teaches art as therapy as well as taking commissions as an illustrator. She also does tree work with Mat. 'I've got quite good with a chainsaw, now!' she laughs.

They met when they were both working at Glastonbury festival; she was part of the catering team that cooked for the building crew. He messaged her sometime later when she was back at the flat she rented in London to ask if she'd consider illustrating a book of poetry he'd written. 'He came up to see me and Baby, my cat, slept on Mat's head all night, which was an indication, I think, that he belonged with us. There was a weirdly instant connection that didn't feel weird, if you see what I mean?'

He invited her to come and visit him, although he warned her that his living conditions were basic. 'I grew up in the countryside,' she told him. 'I'm fine with basic.'

'But this was proper basic! The was no caravan then. There was a very damaged old shepherd's hut that someone Mat had worked for said he could have. We slept on a blow-up mattress on the floor for three weeks. "You're such a bloke!" I told him. "Let's make this place nice!" So we built a bed. We made a door. Gave it a new roof. I painted it. The other shelter, the one he'd built as a kitchen, was no more than functional. I made it more cosy and homely, created a space we could sit around the firepit in the evenings.'

Mat had invited Lauren to stay for a couple of weeks. She stayed for three months on that first visit. 'I ended up taking over. It's just what I do,' she confesses. 'I'm like my mum. Her attitude has always been, "Right – this space has got to be home!" It's got to be nice. It's got to feel comfortable. You deserve to live beautifully. There's nothing wrong with that, nothing wrong with having beautiful things around you and feeling inspired by them every day.'

Lauren's mother is something of a serial homemaker. She

separated from Lauren's father when Lauren was 6 months old and moved 14 times before Lauren left home at 18.

'Mum has always been very good at making a home. Even though I've never lived in the house she lives in now, it still feels like my home when I visit.' I look at this young woman who gives every impression of being thoroughly grounded and unaffected by such a transient existence and wonder whether she's not just very good at hiding the scars of a life lived as a piece of human flotsam.

'It set me up to be very resilient and very good at packing!' she laughs. 'But I'm also not very good at letting go of things. I'm an artist. I draw inspiration from my home, wherever it is, so I collect things, things that I deem interesting or beautiful. I have lots of bones! But it's mostly pictures and stuff people have given me or made for me. My dad gave me this table. The easel is one of the first things Mat gave me.'

The chair I'm sitting on and her desk, together with the table, her treasures and her cat, travel with her wherever she goes. 'I got very good at carting things around when I was growing up. Every time we moved, we'd load up a van with all our stuff, take it out at the other end and Mum would then spend days cleaning and arranging and making our new house beautiful and homely.'

It was the familiar that made Lauren feel each new, unfamiliar house was home: the same curtains, the same sofa, the same pictures hung in a certain way. Her grandparents' house made her feel the same. She spent a lot of time with them when she was growing up. She tells me about their wonderful garden where they grew almost all their own food; they made tipis for her to play in and she climbed trees and made camps. They have now moved to live in the annexe of Lauren's mother's house, but their furniture is the same furniture they've had since Lauren was born. 'And it's the smell of freesias! My grandmother loves freesias and always has them in her house. That smell is home for me too.'

When Lauren left to do an art foundation course in London before going to art school, she lived in a shared house and, like Mat, hated it. 'I love my family and I love my friends, but – and I've inherited this from my father – I don't like people!' The places she felt most at home were places that she could personalise, put her creative stamp on, fix up and decorate. And places where she could see trees . . .

Which is perhaps why she loves living here with Mat so much. It's not an easy lifestyle, though. Her first winter was a challenge. They didn't have the caravan then, just the draughty, unheated shepherd's hut and the open-fronted shelter to cook in. There is no electricity or running water and after weeks of rain, mud, snow and bitter cold, Lauren admitted defeat. 'It was so cold I couldn't function. I couldn't work. It wasn't a home; it was a punishment!' They went to stay with friends and Mat's parents until the spring.

Mat gave Lauren free rein to make the woods somewhere they could both live comfortably. When they got the caravan, they sited it not where he imagined they might one day build a more permanent structure, but in the spot it is in now, beneath a big tree with sprawling, twisted roots, right in the heart of the woods, where Lauren has already imagined the cabin they will build if and when they get permission. 'There will be a sitting room downstairs with a wood burner in the middle and then upstairs a big, sociable kitchen and a little den and our bedroom. And it'll have stained glass windows and be full of beautiful things! There will be a boot room and somewhere to store all our tools and work stuff. And we'll have a separate studio where I can paint and Mat can write. It's going to be very pretty and very homely. I'll have a garden to grow veggies so, along with the pigs and chickens we've got already, we should be able to provide most of our food too.'

For the time being, though, home is the caravan. It's small, just 3.5 metres long and 2 metres wide, but it's got a bed, a little kitchenette and, most importantly, it's warm. But she admits that off-grid living is hard, saying that it is often romanticised but the realities are very different. They have very little indoor space, so when the weather is bad, it's hard to get anything dry. They have no running water, so have to heat water to wash in and are reliant on the stream for their supply. But it dries up when there isn't enough rain and they have to go to friends' houses to fill their bottles. 'It's just very hard work. All the day-to-day things you take for granted take longer, need more thinking about and planning, but when the weather's good, it is the best thing ever – the freedom we feel, living a life so connected with nature.'

Just for fun, Lauren and her mum once added up the number of places Lauren had lived in her 29 years. It came to 32. Living here has made Lauren realise that although her family and her precious things have always made her feel happy and secure wherever she's lived, that she has always felt at home, what she's missed is being stationary. 'I just want one home that stays where it is. I think the idea of putting down roots is very important. I've finally found a place where I can do that. I didn't realise I wanted it, I was missing it, until now. If anyone tells me to leave, I'll fight them tooth and nail. This is home.'

The Cuckoo

———

In the dark depths of winter, I yearn for the April mornings when my walk with the dogs through the nearby woods and heathland is accompanied by the two-note call of a male cuckoo. Sometimes the call is so distant that I have to stop and strain my ears to reassure myself I haven't imagined it. It is a sound that makes me smile, makes my heart leap and my pulse quicken. It is the sound of spring.

The cuckoo's association with the longed-for end of winter makes us feel more benevolent than we might towards a bird that, uniquely in Britain, is entirely self-serving at the expense of other birds. The ultimate free spirit, cuckoos migrate to Britain from west and central Africa simply to mate and lay eggs. Neither male nor female will bother scouting out the perfect nest site or labour to collect material to build or line a nest. They rely on other birds to do that for them, usually dunnocks, reed warblers or meadow pipits. But they don't commandeer the nests; they are not looking for a home where they can safely and cosily bring up their young. They leave that responsibility to the nest builder.

Once she has mated, the female cuckoo will lay anything up to 25 eggs – significantly more than most birds – but she will lay each one in a different nest. Birds are not as bird-brained as we make out. A bird that finds an egg in its nest that differs from its own will throw it out, so the female cuckoo chooses carefully, picking the nest of the species that raised her and whose eggs she can mimic so closely her deception will – usually – go undetected. But she has to act quickly and with stealth. She spies on her target nest, hidden and silent, until both adults are away. When her chance comes, she swoops down, removes one of the existing eggs from the clutch (birds can count), lays her own to replace it and, in just ten seconds, is gone. There is no hanging around to check on whether her chosen foster parents do a good job. As soon as the tasks of breeding and egg laying are over, she, like the male cuckoo (who she will probably never see again), hightail it back to Africa to carry on a life of unfettered, rootless singledom.

Her egg will be conscientiously incubated by the unwitting host bird, hatching, crucially, a few hours before its own eggs. This gives the cuckoo chick the advantage over its 'siblings'. Using its beak, it will systematically remove the other eggs from the nest. If any have hatched, the hatchlings won't be spared either. The cuckoo chick won't rest until it has the whole nest – and all the food the parents bring – to itself. It gets away with this audacious act because its begging call mimics the calls of a whole nest full of hungry chicks, and the adult birds' instincts are so hard-wired to react that they just keep feeding it. It will fledge in three weeks, by which time it is bigger than both its adopted parents, but they continue to feed it for another two weeks, by which time it is independent.

The cuckoo chick will never see its biological parents. They are, by now, long gone. It too will migrate, relying not on parental guidance, but on the Earth's magnetic field and the stars, leaving its birthplace for the forests of Africa.

A Long Walk

I pull into the cul-de-sac and scan the numbers on the doors, but
fail to find the one I'm looking for. I park and find a narrow
walkway tucked between a building and a thick, high hedge. The
house is at the end. Secluded and hidden from view. I ring the bell.
The door is answered by a woman of about my age, small-framed
with delicate features and pale blonde hair tied back and held
away from her face with a hairband.

'Come in,' she smiles. 'I've just got back from dropping my son
off at school.'

The space beyond the hall is bright, clean and uncluttered, the
colours neutral, making the green of the house plants that flank
the doors to the garden and adorn shelves and tables in the
kitchen and sitting room seem particularly rich and intense. 'I do
love my plants,' she laughs. 'I used to have dogs but plants are
easier to look after! I nurture them constantly and they bring me
a lot of joy.'

'They make the house feel very calm,' I say. She looks

slightly surprised by this, as if it wasn't something she'd ever considered.

We sit at either end of the big brown leather sofa. She tucks her legs beneath her and takes a breath. 'I feel like I'm walking through a story that I'm waiting to end,' she says.

The story begins in 1969 in a town on the Dorset coast. The daughter of a prominent, respectable Jewish family was discovered to be pregnant. She was 15 years old. Scandalised, her parents took her out of school and kept her hidden in her bedroom until her baby was due. In the same Dorset town, a 30-year-old woman and her husband of 10 years were being told by a gynaecologist that they would be unable to conceive, news that affected them both deeply. There was a solution, the gynaecologist said. Adoption. He happened to have a patient who was young, unmarried and expecting a child. She would not be keeping it.

In April 1970, the baby was born. A girl. Tiny, with big brown eyes and wisps of pale blonde hair. Solicitors had already drawn up the paperwork – this was a private adoption, allowable in those days – and when the infant girl was nine days old, she was handed over to the delighted couple. Their lives were complete. They named the little girl Lara and she was, they told everyone joyfully, proudly, an idyllic baby, who never cried or acted up, and who would sit quietly and apparently content for hours at a time. But what they believed to be positive signs were quite the opposite.

'I was in a state of shock and trauma.' I look at Lara, questioning. What can she mean? 'It is an all-too-common misconception,' she says, before I can ask. 'If a baby is adopted in the first few days of its life, most assume it will have no knowledge or memory of any other mother or family. I was a "vanilla baby" – the perfect solution for a childless couple. Untainted and unshaped. Except that I wasn't.'

Lara's parents never hid from their daughter the fact that she was adopted. They knew someone who had become totally derailed when told as an adult that she was not biologically related to her family and they were determined not to make the same mistake. So when Lara was barely four years old, her mother told her that unlike the baby that she was now carrying in her tummy – she had, it turned out, been able to conceive after all – Lara had grown in someone else's tummy. Lara remembers the conversation with astonishing clarity almost half a century later.

'We were in my parents' bedroom. It had that velvety flock wallpaper and there were lots of drapes and swags. My mother was sitting on the floor – she liked sitting on the floor – and I was perched up on the corner of their bed. My mother was sorting through her jewellery – she had lots of big, chunky costume jewellery which she kept in plastic bags – and as she was telling me that I was actually someone else's child, she was untangling necklaces and repacking them, as if what she was telling me was completely normal and inconsequential.' And although, Lara concedes, she didn't – and couldn't have – fully understood the meaning of her mother's words, over the coming days and weeks and months and years she processed them.

'I came to the realisation that there was someone else out there who *is* my mother. My real mother. And it made sense to me. I wasn't surprised. Because I always felt I was in the wrong place. That what was supposed to be my home, wasn't. And I didn't feel a connection with my mum. She was always quite strict and quite cold. Even when she was telling me I was adopted, she didn't feel the urge to sit beside me, to hold me or hug me or give me the reassurance I so needed. I think she really believed she was doing the right thing by not making it a big deal, by not making a fuss, but what it proved was that she had no real maternal instinct towards me. That there was no real bond between us. If I needed comfort, if I needed to feel safe, I went to my dad.'

Lara's sense of disconnection, even at such an early age, might well have been compounded by the way her parents made their living. They would buy a house in a poor state of repair, live in it while they did it up, then sell it six months or so later. 'We'd live in an absolute shit-tip, then as soon as it was done and I had a really nice bedroom, the house would go on the market and off we'd go again. It became something of a family joke that by the time I left home I'd lived in 34 different houses. But it wasn't a joke for me. I hated it.' So she retreated into her head – so much so, she says, that where they were physically living became immaterial. Home for Lara wasn't a house. It became instead a quest, a search for something that represented some sort of belonging.

When Lara was in her early teens, the family moved to Alicante in Spain and Lara's relationship with her mother became more and more problematic. 'I couldn't really be in the same space as her and we had a lot of really painful times. I created, instead, a fantasy home in my head, with my biological mum. I imagined what she might be doing, what she might be like, what she might be thinking about me. I imagined the siblings I might have. But at the same time, I had this horrible sense of being rejected. I had been given away by my birth mother. And it made me crave belonging. Crave being accepted. Crave unconditional love. And as I didn't feel I could get those from my family, I turned to boys instead. I thought if I was getting attention from boys, it was a sign that I was OK and that I was accepted. But one of the common complications for people who are adopted is that although they crave attachment, they don't know how to handle it. Don't know what to do with it. Soon after I started a relationship, I would get panicked and anxious. I'd be overwhelmed with fear that I would be left alone, so I would end it. I started to hate myself, to feel worthless. I was a square peg in a round hole. I was in the wrong place but I didn't know how to find the place where I truly belonged.'

Her parents returned to England, leaving the family dog with Lara, who had moved in with a boyfriend and decided to stay in Spain. She was, by now, bilingual and she loved the way of life. Loved being outdoors. The light. The warmth. She moved to Barcelona and got a job. She and her boyfriend got engaged. But the commitment terrified her. 'Home was synonymous with the relationship I was in and the mental state it induced. It was never a constant. It was either a place where I felt calm or stressed and there was nothing in between. I couldn't separate my emotions from where I was living. And when I got engaged, I remember feeling I was being sucked into something I wasn't able to deal with, and I was terrified. And then our dog died. It was the catalyst that made me realise I had to get away from the life I was in. I had to go back to England. And I've never been averse to change. I think with every new change or every new start, there's hope.'

It wasn't long after her return that she found herself in another relationship. He was a man, she tells me with a wry grin, who was not to her parents' liking, but he made her feel wanted and safe. When they met, he didn't have a job and was living a fairly hand-to-mouth existence, but then he found work, a job that paid well and gave him stability. Her new start seemed to be exactly what she needed to do. He and Lara got married and bought a house together. She was 21.

'I took great pride in doing it up. I painted it – even tried doing the tiling myself. It was the early 1990s – a time of pastel colours and dado rails! I wanted it to be entirely different from my parents' space. It was mine and I wanted it to feel like mine,' Lara remembers. For the first time, she created a retreat outside her head, somewhere she felt more stable. Somewhere she could close the door and shut out the world. It felt like a sense of achievement. She had her dogs with her. It was as close to a home as she had ever had, but the emotional attachment still wasn't there. She still didn't feel she belonged. And she knew she would only feel that when she found her biological mother.

*

The letter dropped on to the mat. Lara had spent the last few mornings waiting for the post. Waiting for this handwritten letter that would change everything. Lara's adopted mother may not have been able to give her the physical affection and reassurance that she longed for, but she did show how much she cared for her adopted child in another way: doggedly trawling the electoral roll, making phone calls pretending to be someone else. And in this way, she finally located Lara's birth mother and gave Lara her address. Lara had written to her and, when the handwritten envelope dropped onto her mat, knew that she had replied.

'I didn't sit down. I just read it there and then, standing by the door. She wrote that she always thought about me on my birthday. That she had never stopped wondering about me and that she would love to meet up.' Over the course of a few more letters, they made a plan to meet on Bournemouth pier. Lara's eyes cloud with tears. 'I look so different from the family I grew up with. My dad was part Italian. My mum had jet black hair, which my sister inherited. They are tall. I'm small and blonde and because I look so different from them, I always felt different from them. I just wanted to see someone who looked like me. I truly believed that if and when I did, my whole world would make sense.'

The woman at the end of the pier was irrefutably Lara's biological mother: the similarities between them were instantly apparent. Not just their petite build, their blonde hair, their faces – more surprising and unexpected were their mannerisms. The way they played with their hair. The way they moved. They were identical. For over two decades, Lara had felt rootless and cast out. She had had no sense of where she belonged, of where home was. She had created a home in her head, one whose foundations were built on the knowledge that somewhere was a woman to whom she belonged. And now, she had found her. The meeting went well and it filled Lara with hope. They arranged to meet again, and they did, several times.

Lara travelled to Bristol where her mother lived and her mother loved having her there, revelled in going out with Lara to bars and clubs, enjoyed the fact that everyone thought they were sisters. But Lara didn't want a sister. She wanted a mother. 'The problem was we were so close in age – she's only 16 years older than me – and she just wasn't what I expected or had imagined. She was in a long-term relationship but not married and didn't want to be. Nor did she want children. Having me had traumatised her. I'd had a huge impact on her life. So after the initial excitement of finding each other, of recognising ourselves in each other, I began to realise that the dream I'd had for so long – for years and years – of finding a family and a home that was really mine, that was really where I belonged, was just that. A dream. A fantasy. Because she didn't feel maternal towards me. How could she? Why should she? She chose to give that chance away. She didn't want to be a mother.'

But there was still something she could give Lara that no one else could. 'So many of us who have been adopted just want to know where we come from, and the final piece of my story was to know who my father was. But she wouldn't tell me. She wouldn't talk about it. And so that sense of belonging that I had been looking for all my life, that I had dreamed of and had unwittingly assumed my mother would be able to give me, still eluded me.'

Hurt, angry and desperately upset, Lara felt let down by the one person on whom she had pinned all her hopes. She and her mother drifted apart and eventually stopped seeing each other altogether. Lara's marriage crumbled. It was a desperate time. 'I didn't know where to go or what to do next. I didn't know what the answers were. Nothing I had tried had worked. Nothing made me feel better. My boyfriends didn't work. My family didn't work. Meeting my mother didn't work. I shifted all my hopes onto finding my father, believing he would be the one to hold the answer to who I am and where I belong.' But she didn't know where to start. She had no information at all. Not even a name.

Anyone meeting her at this time, she said, would have imagined she had a perfect life – 'I was very good at putting up a front.' She'd come from a stable, secure background, with parents who had had successful careers, who had given her a good education and all the material things that she needed. She had a good job. She had a house. But it was a thin façade that masked a continuing series of failed relationships, of constant moves, of increasingly desperate attempts to find where she fitted in and where she could settle. She married again. Twice. And she gave birth to a daughter of her own who she named Mia – 'It's Spanish for mine.'

Becoming a mother marked something of a turning point. 'At first, I felt hugely overwhelmed. I didn't know if I had the ability to be what every child deserves. I didn't know if I could commit unwaveringly. I'd never managed it with anything or anyone before. But then, I hadn't known a love like the one I had for Mia and later for my son Kai. It showed me something I never knew I was capable of.' And although the relationships with her children's fathers didn't last, she strived to create a home for them that was like the one she dreamed of for herself. One built on security and love, free of the guilt that she has carried with her since birth. The guilt of being born to someone who didn't want her. The guilt of feeling unable to be the daughter she felt her adopted parents had expected and longed for.

But Lara's own place of sanctuary and security still eluded her. Her search for her father continued without success. Her biological mother had finally relented and told Lara how she became pregnant, but gave her no details that would help her track her father down. Eventually, Lara gave up. She had too little to go on. Occasionally, she would think she had found something, only to have her hopes dashed. It was, she says, too heartbreaking to continue. She began to understand that she couldn't rely on finding her father to give her the anchor she needed to feel settled and rooted. Nor could she rely on a relationship.

She found herself living alone in a house she and her partner had planned to share when he returned from working overseas, but they had split up, leaving her and her children in a house that felt too big and often very lonely. Respite came from its garden, from transforming a forgotten, neglected corner into a joyful riot of hollyhocks and foxgloves, daisies and poppies. She grew shrubs from seed and trawled gardening books for inspiration and information, determined to surround herself with flowers all year round. It was the garden that became her sanctuary: a place of new life and new hope.

Hard as those years were, she looks back on that time as being pivotal. Transformative. In the past, she would have looked to find someone to help her escape her feeling of isolation; now she turned to her garden and to study. She took a degree in psychology, reasoning that the many challenges and traumas she had had to deal with could be harnessed to help other people. Others who, like her, felt different. Felt like they too didn't belong. She found a way to accept herself and, with that acceptance, began, finally to gain the feeling of stability that had been elusive her entire life. And when, after eight solitary years, she met Joel, it felt like the first time she had entered into a relationship because she wanted to, rather than needed to.

It was Joel who persuaded her to rethink giving up on her quest to find her father, to give the one thing she hadn't tried a go: to trace him through a DNA match. Her birth mother had confirmed that Lara's father didn't know about her, and Lara wanted him to know that she existed. She felt that if he knew about her, it would unveil, finally, the answer to where Lara belonged.

In 2019, the DNA agency sent letters to two men, one in Lowestoft and one in Poole. The letter stated that the agency had been contacted by a family member who showed a very close DNA match to both men and that she would like to meet them or get in touch if they were willing. There was no reply from the man in Lowestoft but the man in Poole wrote straight back and said yes.

He was called Tony. He lived in a house Lara had driven past many times in her life, just around the corner from her own. But he wasn't her father. He was her uncle. Her father was Tony's estranged brother, Gerry, who had been living in Lowestoft, but had died just four months before Lara traced him. When she first learned that he was dead, that she had missed meeting him by a matter of months, Lara was in despair, her hopes dashed. Tony offered to help and requested a copy of his brother's will. There was the name of someone with whom Lara's father had shared much of his life but never married. Lara went to meet her and was able to learn about the small details that she felt really identified this man called Gerry as her father, the things that made him tick. The nuances and habits that were part of him; the things that were tricky and annoying. And things they had in common. She discovered that he too struggled to connect with other people. That he was a bit of a loner. Interested in philosophy. And that he'd had a love of cars. 'Something else I share! I'd been interested in cars since I was 14. I knew almost every make and model on the road. My son's the same. I saw so much of myself in what my father's friend described, and that was enough. It was the final piece of the jigsaw puzzle I'd been trying to finish all my life.'

For so many years, Lara had been stuck in the maze of her lost identity. She had no idea where she was going because she had no idea where she belonged. The family she lived with and the houses she lived in were not truly hers and she always felt like an outsider. Always felt different. Only now that she has pieced together her story can she begin to imagine a life that isn't one long restless search. She has done her best for her children. She and Joel are still together – 'A bit of a record for me!' – and perhaps most important of all, she has found a place where she can be at peace with the woman who raised her. 'I've seen now that she is really amazing. I made her life hell and that's not what she thought she was getting, but she stood by me all the way. She accepts me and my story and I accept and love her.'

Lara is now a psychotherapist. She specialises in helping people who struggle with identity issues, anxiety, loss and relationships, and with the mental challenges she understands all too well that can come from being adopted. 'What I experienced is not often talked about or considered. People imagine that adoption is always a positive solution for a child that has been born in less-than-ideal circumstances. But it can often leave them with the unanswered question of "Where do I belong?" and until they can answer that, they will often feel rootless and adrift.'

'And what about you?' I ask. 'Do you feel settled now? Do you feel at home in this house?' She and Joel have lived here for two years.

'We bought it because it was a practical fix,' she says. 'Right size for our children, right location, right price. But it's not somewhere we'll stay. It's a stepping stone.'

'To where?'

'When I know that my children are healthy and happy and independent, then I will find the place that I now know will make me feel truly at home. It will be in Spain. I need sunshine. And a mountain view. There is something about the solidity of a mountain. It brings peace and sanctuary. It's reliable. It's unmoving.'

The Hermit Crab

––––

The hermit crab is neither a hermit nor even a true crab. True crabs can grow their own shells, whereas hermit crabs rely on other animals – sea snails like whelks and periwinkles – to provide shells for them.

A hermit crab is a curious and not very beautiful creature. Its hairy, spidery legs and pincer-style claws are the most crab-like thing about it. The rest of its body, usually hidden away, is like that of a prawn, with maybe a bit of scorpion thrown in. It has the unhealthy-looking pallor of something that rarely sees daylight – and it rarely does. The tail end is particularly muscular and tends to curve under itself.

Without a shell, a hermit crab's chances of survival are slim. In the tropics, the fierce sun would soon cook that soft, pale body, and everywhere hermit crabs exist – and that's most parts of the world – there are many other animals that want to eat them. So, a shell is vital for protection. They just have to find the right one because not just any old shell will do.

A hermit crab will size up a potential shell: tapping it, smelling it, checking out the entrance, assessing any damage. It must be the perfect size, shape and weight because anything other than perfect will compromise the crab's life expectancy. Once satisfied, it will move in, using the muscular end of its body to attach itself to the shell's inside column, and there it will stay, safe and self-contained, until the shell becomes too small.

When regular crabs become too big for their shells, they moult. Their existing shell will start to split open, like the shirt of the Incredible Hulk, revealing a soft, new shell, more appropriate to the crab's increased size, beneath. There is one disadvantage to being able to provide your own shell as and when you need it, and that is, once exposed, the new shell offers no protection at all. It needs time to harden, which means the crab has to find somewhere safe to hide and go without food until its armour is in full working order.

When a hermit crab outgrows its shell, it simply has to find another one to move into. But that's not always easy. Empty shells are often few and far between, and it is likely that other crabs will also be on the lookout for a new home too. Competition can be fierce: hermit crabs have been seen to kill each other over a shell. Some make do – using discarded tins, plastic bottles and other human detritus left on beaches – often with fatal results. But biologists have also observed hermit crabs forming what they call a 'vacancy chain'.

An empty shell, as we know, is a valuable resource and will attract crabs from all over the beach, like wasps to jam. The crabs aren't just coming for a viewing; they need to move. All of them will have outgrown their current shells, but the vacant shell won't be right for all of them. The clever crabs know this and come to an arrangement. They form a queue in order of size and, once the crab that deems the vacant shell perfect moves in, leaving its own shell empty, the smaller crab next in line moves into that empty shell, and so on. It is the hermit crabs' way of moving up the property ladder.

Where Is Home . . .?

James Greenwood describes himself as a property doctor. His 'patients' are people who want to find somewhere to live, who understand the enormous importance of getting it right but are confused or fearful about making the wrong decision. Which is something that happens surprisingly often, James tells me, when they go it alone without his help. People will buy a house – not first-time buyers looking to get on the property ladder but people at the stage of life when they are looking for the sort of house they can stay in long term, raise a family in – and two years later, that house will come on the market again. 'And it is almost always because they haven't thought things through. Haven't worked out what constitutes home for them.'

So that's what James does: he helps his clients work out what encapsulates their idea of the perfect home, a place they can stay in at least until their children, if they have them, have finished their education and left. The importance of stability and grounding can't, in his view, be overstated. 'It's not great for business if everyone stays in the house we find them for 30 years! But it's a good indication that I've done my job well. Moving is so disruptive, so unsettling and expensive, that no one should do it more than they have to, particularly if children are involved.'

He will often start a search by going to see his clients in their current home. And if he is helping find somewhere for a couple, he makes sure both of them are there. Because however happy a relationship, and however much a couple may appear to agree on everything, more often than not, James will discover that what they *actually* want from a home can differ wildly. So he tries to build up a picture of how they live and what's important to them.

He'll ask about family – whether they need or want to be close to relatives. He'll enquire about children and schooling and hobbies. How do they like to spend their time when they are not working? Do they entertain? Do they like to cook? Do they enjoy being outside? Right down to the nitty gritty, like what side of the bed they like to sleep on. He'll encourage them to see a lot of houses: 'The biggest mistake is not seeing enough. Finding the right thing is hard work, but given the investment, both financial and emotional, it's worth putting the effort in. It will never be home if it doesn't make you feel happy and safe. And, funnily enough, nobody ever buys what they think they are going to.'

James certainly didn't envisage buying the house that he and his family have lived in for the last 27 years. Not only was it in a part of the country where neither he nor his wife Carina knew anybody or had any sort of connection, more fundamentally, the building wasn't – and had never been – a home. It had been a small hotel. A very bad one. James knows this because he and Carina stayed in it while they were house hunting. 'We had the most awful Fawlty Towers night of no hot water and deep-fried food that was still frozen in the middle. It was just a shocker.' But they had rather liked the house they had seen for sale nearby, so arranged a second viewing.

When they returned, they drove past the hotel. Perhaps unsurprisingly, it had gone bankrupt, was boarded up and on the market. They realised almost instantly that they were more excited by the thought of living in the hotel – despite its bad associations – than the house they had come back to see. 'We were seduced by the fact that it had more space than we ever thought we could afford and we both liked the idea of a project – of turning it into a home. But most of all, it had an incredible view, one of the best I'd ever seen – and I'd seen a fair few on my travels.'

This isn't an idle boast. At the age of 24, James set off to travel around the world. On his own. On a horse. For a decade, he lived an entirely itinerant life, returning to the UK for a couple of months each year. During one of those return visits, he met and fell in love with Carina, although he continued his journey even after they were married and had their first child. When his odyssey was nearing its end and they had another child on the way, they faced the very same conundrum that James has been helping people solve ever since: where and what is home?

James had had more opportunity to ponder this than most. He spent thousands of nights when he was on the road either alone in his tent or a cheap hotel room, where he had only himself to consider but loneliness to contend with. Then there were many other times when he had an introduction or met someone along the way who invited him to stay with them. When he was a guest in someone else's home, although he would be grateful for their hospitality, he never felt he could really relax and would worry that he was an imposition. What he keenly missed in those situations was what he describes as 'the quiet privacy so valued by the British'. And staying with someone isn't always less lonely. He longed for his community – not necessarily people he knew, but people who shared his language and his cultural references. Those small, seemingly insignificant things you have in common: watching the same TV programmes, growing up listening to the top 40, spending your pocket money on Woolworths' pick and mix. They appear frivolous and inconsequential but are potent and strong indicators of where and with whom we fit. Not that when he returned, James set about finding a neighbourhood where the only people who lived there had fond memories of *Bagpuss*, Curly Wurlys and *The Beano*, but it narrowed his search down to the country where he felt most at home – and that was the UK, where he'd grown up.

That sense of belonging is a powerfully emotive force and feeling at home is impossible without it, as a friend discovered when going to visit her father. Alzheimer's had made him too vulnerable to be able to stay in his own house and his family had had to persuade him, much against his will, to move into a care home.

They had carefully chosen items to take with him to make his new room feel as familiar and homely as possible. Pictures and photographs, his favourite chair, his bedspread, items of clothing and books he loved. But those treasured things weren't enough. In a heartbreaking exchange, the old man, for a moment lucid, declared that he wanted to go home. 'What is it about here that isn't home, Dad?' my friend asked. 'Belonging,' he said.

'Not belonging is a terrible feeling,' wrote American author Phoebe Stone in her novel *The Romeo and Juliet Code*. 'It feels awkward and it hurts, as if you were wearing someone else's shoes.'

To belong, according to the dictionary, is to be connected; to be a member or part of something. Or to be an inhabitant, accepted by a group or society. But it is also that intangible, visceral feeling that is really only obvious in its absence; when you have the sensation of being adrift or lost. When you cast around for the familiar and can't find it.

Buildings can – and often do – evoke a strong emotional response. Walk into one of Europe's great medieval cathedrals and it is hard not to feel both cowed and overawed by that hushed cavernous opulence. Frank Gehry's gloriously improbable design for the Guggenheim Museum in Bilbao appears to cheat all architectural rules, inciting an exuberant wonder upon its visitors. The slave castles on Ghana's coast chill and horrify. At the University of Coimbra in Portugal, the Joanina Library wraps all who enter in a heavy velvet cloak of leather-bound delight. Our response to domestic spaces can be just as affecting and, if we are considering living in them, possibly an indication of whether we will be happy doing so. But can you make a building feel like somewhere you belong, even if it doesn't feel that way from the outset? This is another conundrum that James comes up against frequently.

'It is very easy to be put off a house because it doesn't "feel" right,' he says. 'It might have a terrible atmosphere and feel anything but homely, but that isn't a compelling enough reason to write it off immediately.'

My mum would disagree. She is a very strong believer in the feel of a house needing to be right and would have flatly ignored James, as she did my dad, when they were looking for their first house together. She infuriated Dad by absolutely refusing to consider living in the one house they'd seen that was the right size, in the right place and that they could afford. 'It had the most horrible atmosphere,' she said. 'It was a shame, because Dad was right, it was perfect in every other respect, but there was something creepy and unsettling about it and I knew I could never live there.'

She's passed on that belief to me: it doesn't matter what a place looks like, if it doesn't feel right then it's not. Although that philosophy didn't work when it came to choosing our last house in London. Ramshackle and dilapidated as it was, it had a good feeling about it. At least, I thought it did. But for whatever reason, that feeling didn't sustain once we were living there. And I was proved wrong again when James found a house for some friends of mine. They were delighted with the little cottage perched high up on the side of a valley with views over the trees. I went to visit soon after they'd bought it and tried to be delighted too. But internally I was struggling because to me the house felt sad and charmless and cold. I simply couldn't imagine this being their home. Nor did they have the budget to do anything dramatic to the shape or structure of the house that might have made it feel more convivial.

Then, some weeks later, I went back. I couldn't believe I was in the same house. The depressing fog-grey interior had been newly painted in another neutral shade, but one that was bright and warm. There were pictures and books, rugs on the floor, lamps and a squishy sofa. The once-stark kitchen, complete with the air of disregard kitchens have when only the microwave and kettle are used, now had a table, chairs, pots of herbs on the windowsill, fruit in a bowl. But ultimately, that's all just set dressing. What had really changed was the way the house was being lived in. It had gone from plainly functional to what James describes as 'a true home: one that is a reflection of the people who live in it. Both a genial and welcoming space to others, and a private retreat – one you can return to, shut the front door and feel comfortable and safe.'

There's a sign in the utility room as you walk into James's house, hand painted on a rough plank of wood. On one half, 'ASIA 96' is written in red paint with a tick beside it, presumably to commemorate when James finished that leg of his ride around the world. And on the other, in black marker pen, is a stick drawing of a pregnant woman holding the hands of a child. They are standing beside a house, drawn as a triangle topping a rectangle in which four evenly spaced black squares are grouped around a bigger black square, representing windows and a door. Above it are written the words 'WELCOME HOME!!'.

I never saw this house in its previous incarnation as an abandoned hotel, but there is no hint, no lingering sense of its former unloved, unwelcoming persona. It is spacious, but in no way echoey or grand, and it achieves all the things that James considers constitute a true home. Its heart is right in the middle of the building. The kitchen is here, with its crammed shelves, mugs on hooks and solid old range. There's a big square table, its scrubbed wood bearing the rings and marks of many a gathering, surrounded by benches with soft, faded cushions. The other half of the space is arranged around the fireplace. It is flanked by bookshelves, floor to ceiling – a glorious, inviting jumble of words that would make a librarian swoon. There are faded sofas, baggy and inviting. Paintings and plants sit alongside candles stuck in bottles with solidified waterfalls of wax tumbling down their sides. And there's the view. It is of the Severn Estuary, a wide expanse of tidal water that merges with the sky, creating a diorama of ever-shifting light and colour and texture that fills the windows and has an almost gravitational pull. It transfixes. Holds you in its thrall.

James's children are grown up now and have left their family home to begin the search for their own homes, wherever and in what form they may be. Which leaves James and Carina with the familiar conundrum of those whose households have shrunk and whose practical requirements for a home have changed. They've talked about what they might do with the liberation they now have.

'If you did go,' I ask, 'what would you take with you that could make you feel similarly at home elsewhere?'

'Oh, I could just saddle up and go,' James says breezily, 'because the things that make this home, we can't take with us. When I drive to our local town through the lanes, past the houses and the farms that I have been passing for nearly three decades, I know why a gate might be open or shut. We are connected to this place; we have our network, our community. And the thing we value most about our house is the view. And we can't take that.'

And so they are going to stay.

... And What's Inside it?

———

Shortly after we moved to Wales, we discovered the store owned and run by Mark and Sally Bailey. It's in an unlikely setting: not in a town, or near any other shops, but in the barns and outbuildings of what was once a farm, still surrounded by fields and barely visible from the road. The entrance is through high glass and metal doors which lead into the side of the main barn. But before you even get that far, there will be a collection of objects outside the door that catch the eye: old apple crates; tarnished, slightly battered metal buckets or wooden trays of flowerpots, the orange of the terracotta softened by age and lichens. And they will be displayed in that apparently random, careless way that is almost impossible to emulate, so that they don't look like objects for sale. Just things you wish you could have.

Inside, the space is huge, yet somehow doesn't feel cavernous. Nor does it feel like a shop. Although they are selling homewares, Sally and Mark haven't attempted to make it look like the inside of a house: there are no mock-ups of rooms suggesting how pieces of furniture and accessories might go together. But it does feel like walking through someone's – albeit huge – home. It is a combination of the way things are laid out and mixed up – things that are purely practical, like balls of string on wooden spindles, alongside more decorative objects or curiosities, like vintage wooden shoe lasts (I bought one which I use as a door stop) and glove hangers – and the feeling that everything in there has been carefully considered and chosen; that this is a curated collection of much-loved things that might well be in Mark and Sally's actual home too. Books, lamps, slubby linen aprons in soft, muted colours. Enamel plates, wooden bowls, bottles of oil and tins of spices. Vintage trowels, wooden dominoes, plants, candles, soaps, chocolate. Generously wide sofas, quirky one-off chairs and stools and tables. Baskets, lampshades, ceramics and exquisitely carved wooden acorns . . . And the displays and the collection are always changing.

'Mark was here at 4.30 this morning,' Sally tells me. We're sitting on the mezzanine overlooking the main shop floor, on one of the dangerously comfortable sofas. 'He's usually here at that time, just looking at things, changing things, redoing things. I don't know whether you've seen it yet, but yesterday he decided to renew the cart shed – paint the entire floor before we opened! I'm telling him it's going to be chaos, but he doesn't take any notice. He just does it.'

Sally grew up in South Wales, not far from Cardiff. Her father worked for British Steel and her mother had a saddler's shop, where Sally helped at weekends and over the holidays. They lived in a row of terraced houses, all architecturally identical to each other, but inside, Sally tells me, their house was very different from those of her friends and neighbours. 'Mum loved old things,' she says, 'so we didn't really have much that was new or modern in the house. She was very into antiques and she'd inherited a few, but she was also clever at reusing and recycling things. She had a good eye for spotting something unusual or seeing the potential in something that others didn't. And she was good with colour too. So home was a bit of a sanctuary. It was warm and cosy and natural. Close the door and you instantly felt comfortable and relaxed.'

Her mother's style and the feeling it evoked was a huge influence on Sally. After leaving college, she got an apprenticeship as an architectural technician at a local firm, doing drawing work. It was there that she started to get interested not so much in the design of the exterior of buildings but in their interiors. The art college in Cardiff was starting a course in product design, which included the design of interiors, and Sally enrolled.

Mark had done an apprenticeship in carpentry and went on to do joinery and cabinetmaking. When he and Sally met, he was running an antiques shop and living above another shop in a small flat. 'It was very much a single bloke's place,' Sally says, laughing. 'One packet of Alpen in the cupboard and nothing else . . .' They moved to a little terraced house after they married and it was then, Sally remembers, that they started to formulate the style and ethos that has been fundamental to their lives and business for the last 40 years – 'Of course, it has developed and been tweaked over that time, but its basis has remained the same.'

Like her mother, Sally didn't want to fill their house with new furniture and mass-produced accessories. She and Mark wanted their home to feel unique to them, to reflect their admiration for good workmanship and design. They intended to use old tiles on the floors, interesting handles on the doors, fixtures and fittings that weren't off the shelf from the local DIY shop. And it was, she said, almost impossible to find these things. So when they did, if they didn't need them for their own house, they would sell them alongside the antiques in Mark's shop.

It was the precursor to the store they have now, and one of the reasons she cites for its enduring appeal and success. 'If we don't like something, we don't buy it and we won't sell it. We've never tried to follow current trends or fashions.' So everything about their store – the lime plaster on the walls, the exposed wooden beams, the recycled flooring, the natural, muted colours and organic shapes – is a reflection of what they feel makes a good home. 'Natural light and good ventilation are key; being able to have open windows, see something green outside. All those things are good for mood and health and a sense of well-being.' It was those factors that made them choose the site they did, even though it was remote and out of the way. And it's those things that have been the deciding factors when choosing to buy the four subsequent houses they have lived in since their first little terrace.

Light and air may be important for a space to feel pleasant to be in, but, just as important, Sally advocates, is living in it for long enough to get a sense of how rooms are going to be used, what works and what doesn't, before making any dramatic changes. Her kitchen, she tells me, is the soul of their house. 'It is somewhere everybody can gravitate towards, and even when Mark and I are there by ourselves, we have a ritual: we set the table, use crockery and glasses we've collected over the years. Relish being in it.'

I feel the same about my kitchen, I tell her. I enjoy the informal sociability it allows. It is a room to gather, talk, eat and drink, but also a room where I can happily be alone, getting on with the gentle, homely routine of preparing food in the company of the dogs, asleep in their baskets or sitting at my feet looking hopeful.

'Comfort is an important aspect of making a house a home too,' Sally says. 'Both physical and emotional. Investing in a good sofa and a great bed – and I do love linen sheets.'

'Aren't they a nightmare to iron?' I ask.

'Oh, I don't iron them, I just leave them crunchy. I quite like them like that! And smell makes a big difference too. I always take candles and my own soap when I'm staying in a hotel, just because I know little things like that, with a familiar smell I love, will make me feel comfortable. It's about creating an ambience that makes you relaxed and at ease: a place of calm where you can shut out the world and switch off entirely.'

It seems obvious, nowadays, that we would want, indeed expect, our homes to be comfortable, but that wasn't always the case. Houses, and the things in them, were once purely functional, something that only really began to change as people started to live differently: when houses became less public and more private, and the space broken up into smaller, more intimate rooms. And that didn't start happening until the seventeenth century. As historian John Lukacs wrote, 'Domesticity, privacy, comfort, the concept of the home and of the family: these are, literally, principal achievements of the Bourgeois Age.'

Ultimately, it is things, Sally says – a candle, or books, or a painting, or a plant – that bring comfort to a room. But they need to be a true reflection of the people who live there: things they love, that make them happy, that make them feel like they belong. It's those more personal objects that elevate a house from simply being a building with furniture and appliances to being a home – 'So often, I'll look at the aspirational houses in magazines or on the TV and they're completely sterile. Everything is carefully placed and contrived. They look too perfect and impersonal. They are show homes. There is nothing comfortable about them.'

But it is, of course, possible to go too far the other way. A room that feels overcrowded and cluttered is rarely comfortable. 'We've always got piles of magazines and newspapers and books, everywhere,' Sally confesses, 'and among the things we have in the house that are very considered and treasured, there is stuff that Mark might have found, or things he's working on or considering. We've got lots of baskets that seem to end up being filled with things that we're not sure what to do with. There is a line between a home that is too tidy and ordered to feel comfortable and one that is just as uncomfortable because it feels chaotic and out of control. So every now and then we'll have a purge. We'll go through things and ask ourselves, 'Do I like that? Do I need it? Does it work? Is it useful? Is it beautiful?'

There are a few things that have followed them from house to house: an old coffer and a small table that had been in Sally's childhood home, which she kept after her mother died. And there are two little carved wooden figures. 'I don't even know where we found them. We've just had them forever. If our house was burning down, they are the things I would grab because if I had them with me, I would feel, even if the place we had to stay wasn't our home, that it could be somewhere we could settle for a while. Light, air and comfort are all important, but ultimately, it is the things that are in a house that make it a home.'

Dara Huang has made a career and built a business based on that philosophy, creating bespoke interiors for the homes of celebrity clients, famous CEOs and billionaires. Having lived in Tokyo, Switzerland, Hong Kong, New York and London, and with a job that involves constant travelling, she describes herself as a 'nomad, a global citizen', but she was born in Florida. Her parents had immigrated from Taiwan, both academics, with modest means and high ideals. They brought nothing with them from their home country, Dara tells me, 'Other than recipes, an Asian work ethic and a strong belief in the power of education.' The house Dara and her sister grew up in was furnished no differently from those of her friends, and, apart from a dinner service, which

Dara remembers had an Asian-influenced design, it was an all-American home. And a very happy one. Dara's abiding memories of her childhood are of growing up in a very loving household. Her father was an engineer and worked for NASA. Her mother had been a teacher in Taiwan but didn't speak English when they arrived in America, so she stayed at home and looked after her family, cooking meals that they would eat together around the table and teaching her daughters to sew. 'My parents are still together to this day. They've set an amazing example to me both with regards to work and family.'

From an early age, Dara loved drawing and art was her abiding passion while growing up. But when it came to choosing a subject for her degree, her parents – 'like most Asian parents!' she laughs – wanted her to choose something that would give her a vocation. 'And I looked down the list of subjects offered by Florida University and chose architecture. I didn't really know what architecture was but it seemed the best option for me on the list!'

Dara's family had moved by then to a house in Orlando. 'It was a beautiful four-bedroomed house, with a swimming pool. I remember my mum got some curtains made and noting how they influenced the whole look and feel of that room, but my university course wasn't anything to do with interiors. I wasn't aware there was such a thing as interior design back then. I was still trying to understand the theoretical basis to architecture.' She obviously got to grips with it pretty well because she left Florida with a top degree and a place at Harvard to do a masters.

She moved into an on-campus house with three roommates and it was in this house that Dara says she made her first attempt at interior design, still without really knowing what that was. 'I just wanted it to look nice when I came home.' They painted the kitchen with zebra stripes and the wall of one room chocolate brown. She bought cheap but stylish wooden furniture from Ikea, put it together with a sisal rug and potted palms, and, thanks to the sewing lessons her mother had given her, made cushions for her bedroom. Her academic work was time-consuming; she spent long hours in the studio. So when she came back to the house, she wanted a place that felt relaxing: 'I wanted it to feel really positive and balanced and uniform. A lot of design is about what feels good, what makes a space feel comfortable, and that's what I was trying to achieve. It's not about money, it's just as much about intuition and taste.'

She did the same when she left Harvard and took a job for a top architectural practice in Switzerland. 'I had student debt and junior architects don't get paid very much, so I didn't have a lot of money to play with. I went back to Ikea and I also discovered "furniture day". On given days people can put furniture they don't want any more out on the street and anyone can take it. And often it's beautiful! So I was mixing Ikea with this amazing old world, mid-century furniture.' Her thrift finds came with her to London when she moved again to join another prestigious firm. 'I always tried to make the best out of the space I was living in. I didn't particularly understand interiors but just felt confident of what I thought looked good.'

It was in London that she decided she wanted to take her career in a slightly different direction – to concentrate more on what could be done inside a building rather than its external structure. She joined a firm that did interior fit-outs for company offices and developments, and started to bring in clients, finding she enjoyed the networking as much as the creative process. In 2013, she decided to set up on her own, her commissions gradually shifting from interior fit-outs to show homes for high-end developers. 'And that's the difference between a house and a home,' she says, echoing the sentiments of Sally Bailey. 'Whatever I did to the interiors, it would still be a house. But the moment the keys were handed to the new owners was the moment when it could become a home. But they needed to add their own stuff – and it doesn't matter what it is. What matters is that every object holds a memory; you know where it comes from; it's personal. Without those things a house will never feel like a home.'

Yet, many of the clients she works for rely, sometimes entirely, on Dara to create a home for them. So she and her team will try to source things with history, that are not new and shiny and polished. They'll choose or make things that are unique and have character. When billionaire Chris Burch asked her to do the interiors of his three homes – one in the Hamptons, one in Miami Beach and the third in New York City – he told her he liked a traditional, old English style, lots of patterns and florals. He came shopping with her to antiques markets in Paris and London and they chose pieces together. He had art works that he wanted her to include and family photographs that he asked to be printed and framed for the various houses. But he is unusual, she tells me. 'Many of the clients who hire us don't have the time or the bandwidth or the knowledge of how to deal with everything. They want to move into a turnkey space. We'll do everything from structural changes, interior design and decorating, right down to buying the cutlery, the clothes hangers, even the toilet brushes! People often want a cosy ambience which we'll achieve with careful lighting, curtains, rugs and throws. They want it to feel homely but they don't have time to do the home-making.'

'So can they ever feel like home, if everything has been chosen for them, if there is nothing that is personal to them? That doesn't have the history you say is so important.'

Dara shrugs and smiles. 'Many of the houses we've worked on won't even be the owners' principal homes. They may spend only a few days or weeks there a year, so yes, a lot of them will feel like show homes.'

'And what about you?' I ask. 'What makes a home for you?'

'Mirrors,' she says. 'I put big mirrors in every room; they make them feel really light and bright. Curtains, to soften a space. Decorative things that may have no purpose or use, but they make me happy. Plants. But ultimately, a house needs a heart. It needs stuff that is connected to the person or people who live there, who know its story. And for me, my photos are the most important thing – seeing my son when he was a baby, the memories that can't be replaced. And the rocks my son and I have collected when we go on holiday. I am one of those people who goes away and comes back with a suitcase full of rocks! We put them in baskets and we know where all of them came from. We do paintings together too, huge linen canvases that decorate all my spaces.'

'And is home London?'

'Home is within. It's where my heart is. And my heart is with my son. Wherever he goes, I go. My home is with him.'

'So, money can't buy a home?' I ask. And Dara laughs.

The Bowerbird

———

I had always believed interior design was something that had come into vogue fairly recently – perhaps in the 1960s when post-world-war austerity was receding. That it came hand in hand with the new fashions, new styles of music, new vibrancy of the age, that it was something of a modern frivolity. But the very conscious curating of the look and feel of the rooms within our houses dates much further back. The idea could even be attributed to one particular woman: Madame de Pompadour.

When Louis XV of France moved his court and government to the Palace of Versailles in 1722, he set about making changes to the way the rooms within the great palace were used. Under his predecessor, Versailles had been a very public place. The idea of a dwelling place being private, or having private spaces within it, hadn't yet developed. Houses, even those of the rich, had gradually evolved from being one main space where everything happened. The hall, as it was known in medieval times, was kitchen, dining room, meeting room, workshop, storeroom and bedroom for the whole household. There were no individual rooms used only for specific purposes and no concept of privacy. Adults, children, servants and guests all slept together in the same room. The houses of the Middle Ages were purely practical shelters with few adornments, little in the way of anything decorative and even less in the way of comfort. Individual rooms, decoration, the desire to sit on something other than the floor or a wooden bench was to come later, as would the idea of home that we recognise today. Even a century or so beyond the Middle Ages, in the many-roomed, richly decorated, plushly furnished Versailles of Louis XIV, courtiers could go everywhere within the palace with few restrictions. The state bedroom, where the king slept, was a public space, with up to a hundred members of the court attending his 'getting-up' ceremony, looking on as he was washed, dressed, shaved and ate breakfast. The same would happen at the end of the day when he went to bed.

But Louis XV started to instigate change, creating a private suite of a mere 50 rooms within the palace, which was small(ish) and more intimate, and where few people were allowed to go. This decision was thought to have been influenced by Madame de Pompadour, briefly his mistress, but his confidante and adviser for over two decades. It was she who encouraged his interest in decoration, in transforming the interiors of his palaces and the houses he built for her into treasure troves with secret passageways and hidden staircases, keeping him enthralled with new, ever more elaborate schemes and ideas. And her influence went beyond the royal household, reaching into the homes of the

Parisian bourgeoisie, encouraging them to create more rooms and private spaces within their houses and to decorate them without restraint. This was the era of the Rococo, where any and every surface was adorned with curls and swirls, with motifs of shells and flowers, painted and gilded and completely over the top.

However, long before a French king's mistress was toying with the latest silks and colour schemes, a bird was creating and decorating spaces to bewitch and delight in the forests of Australia and Papua New Guinea.

The bowerbird is named for the bowers it constructs as part of an elaborate courtship ritual. But it is not the female that goes to the trouble of building these structures, decorating them with flamboyant and considered care in an effort to keep her love interest interested; it is the male. He is constructing a theatre to show off his accomplishments with the shameless hope that his female audience of one will be seduced to such an extent that she'll be unable to refuse him. There are several species of bowerbird and each one brings its own unique design flare to its bower.

Before building can start, the forest floor must be cleared of debris. Sticks are then collected and carefully arranged. Some species push one end of each stick into the ground in opposite rows, angled so they lean towards each other, forming a sort of arched tunnel. Another builds a bower shaped like a Bedouin tent; another, a conical tower. But no theatre is complete without a stage, ideally with an uninterrupted view from a private box. The male's plan, once he has enticed a female to visit his bower and admire his architectural prowess, is to lay on sparkling and unforgettable entertainment, which might include mimicry – 'Listen! Is that a pig playing in a waterfall?' – or performing mesmerising tricks with his eyes, or strutting and posturing like a matador, using his wings as a cape. The great bowerbird, a rather drab, beige, unassuming looking creature, will catch his potential mate's eye by revealing, with a magician's flourish, a shocking pink crest on the top of its head – the avian equivalent of an apparently soberly dressed man taking off his grey overcoat to reveal an extravagantly patterned silk shirt beneath.

But, as any theatre impresario knows, first, you have to persuade your audience to attend your show rather than anyone else's. And the bowerbird does that by making his bower as eye-catching and unmissable as possible, using elaborate decoration. Once again, each species has a signature style. The satin bowerbird, with its glossy blue-black plumage and bright blue eyes, perhaps, unsurprisingly, favours a blue colour scheme to decorate his bower. He'll collect all manner of objects, both natural and manmade – from flowers and feathers to plastic bottle tops and clothes pegs – and, as long as they are blue, they will be arranged and placed with elaborate care on the ground around the bower.

The Vogelkop bowerbird covers his stage with a layer of moss and chooses his decorative objects according to novelty value rather than colour. Some birds lay their treasures out in a very specific order of size, placing the smallest objects close to the bower and the largest further away, creating a forced perspective that will draw and focus the female's attention on her suitor's performance.

If the female is lured by a male's building skills, charmed by his decorative flair, and amused and impressed by his courtship display, she will consent to mate with him. Once he's had his way, the male will leave the female to get on and build her own nest and rear their offspring on her own. He, meanwhile, will return to his bower, make any repairs or adjustments he deems necessary, collect a few more treasures to lay out in a tempting fashion and await the next girl to come along.

A Stuffed Duck and Gold Teeth

────

When your home is all you've ever known and has been in your family since the time of your great-grandfather, it is perhaps harder to define what 'home' is. You take it for granted, in the same way you take your own hands and feet. It is as intrinsic as that. But stability for the Doull family came only after a time of great strife. The infamous Highland clearances of the nineteenth century saw crofts that enabled their tenants to grow food and make a living, as well as providing them with a home, cleared of people, fences and buildings to make way for sheep. Landowners throughout Scotland and the islands, in a quest to make greater profits from their property, saw sheep as more valuable than people, and crofters were often thrown off the land they had lived on for generations with not enough notice to find anywhere else to live.

Willie Doull's great-grandfather was evicted from his home in the west of Shetland and moved to a vacant croft on the island of Muckle Roe off the north-west coast some time, Willie believes, in 1860. He became the tenant of another landlord, renting a small area of land and supplementing his income by fishing. There was a house tucked away between the red rocks and brown-green folds of the hill, looking out over the water of Roe Sound, but it was in a bad state of repair. The first of Willie's ancestors to be born on Muckle Roe was his great uncle Sinclair in 1862, and it is said that when his great-grandmother was giving birth, she could see out through the gaps in the walls into the yard where the hay was kept.

The landlord built a new house on the site for the family – putting the rent up accordingly – in 1864. It was a low house with a thatched roof but was later made higher and given a new felt roof. Willie's mother was born there in 1905 and Willie, the last of the family to be born at home rather than in the maternity hospital in Lerwick, in 1952. By then, the house had been extended out to the side, creating two extra bedrooms for the growing family.

Willie's childhood was spent almost entirely on Muckle Roe, an island about three miles in diameter. He went to the island's little school, sometimes getting a lift in the morning and walking back in the afternoon. His best friend was a boy called Peter, who lived on a neighbouring croft. He remembers just two occasions when he left Muckle Roe as a child: once to visit his aunt on the island of Papa Stour and the other – 'The only time I can remember my parents leaving here' – to see his uncle who was a policeman on the island of Yell.

He left school just before his fifteenth birthday to work with his father at home, as well as doing any other odd jobs that people needed doing – driving tractors or moving sheep. But there wasn't much money about, so there wasn't a huge demand for his services. Many of his contemporaries went to work on ships but Willie never had a wish to go anywhere else. Instead, he got a job as a postman and continued to live in his childhood home.

When he was 18, he started going out with Jacqueline. They had been at secondary school together in the neighbouring village of Brae, but she was three years younger, so they weren't in the same class, and her family lived in the village of Vidlin on the mainland. But her father and the father of Willie's best friend, Peter, were brothers and so she was often at Peter's house, as was Willie. Jacqueline laughs that probably the thing Willie liked about her most was that he didn't have to go very far from his home to see her.

They married in 1974 and Jacqueline came to live at the croft with Willie. Like previous generations, they have expanded and changed the house to fit their family, now two sons, a daughter and seven grandchildren. As Jacqueline shows me around, it strikes me that in the same way that photo albums capture the story of a family over time, this house does the same. From the raising of the roof to each additional room, the house is the physical embodiment of the lives of four generations of Doulls. 'You should see the attic,' she says, a look of amused despair on her face. 'There's so much stuff up there, I wonder the floor doesn't collapse. A telephone repair man came here once and had to go up there to sort out some part of the wiring. For all we know, he might still be there, lost among all the things that have never been thrown away.'

Willie's entire family history is up in that loft. There are boxes of books and drawings Willie did at school; photos going back so many generations that no one is sure who the people in them are – although Jacqueline says it is the photos that she would hold onto above all else. There's a collection of old radios – 'I threw one away once,' Willie recalls, ruefully, 'and regretted it. Not because it was ever going to be worth anything, but you just might need it – or part of it – one day.' Which makes we wonder what he might do with his uncle's gold front teeth, sent home with his other personal effects when he died on a ship, which are also in the attic. And then there's the dunter.

'Dunter' is the Shetland word for an eider – the rather noble-looking sea ducks frequently seen bobbing about near the shore of lochs and bays. The males have striking black and white plumage, whereas the females are an unremarkable and uniform brown, perfect camouflage for a bird that nests on the ground. One of Willie's uncles found a dunter nest when he was a child, took an egg, brought it home and put it under one of the domestic ducks they kept at the croft. The egg hatched and the little eider duck became a member of the family – until natural urges took over and she went off with a male. 'But she came back every year,' Willie says, re-telling this old family story – 'nested on the shore below the house. Then one year she was shot. She wasn't killed outright but made her way back to her nest, where she died. So, my grandparents had her stuffed. She's been up in the attic since between the wars.'

Willie and Jacqueline's home extends beyond the house, beyond its collection of byres and sheds that has also grown with each generation. It stretches beyond the boundaries of their land, encompassing the community of crofters who are as deeply rooted here as they are. The people who live at this end of Muckle Roe are, Willie states, to all intents and purposes extended family, united by the demands of working the land to survive. They share machinery – planters and spinners – and in bygone years helped each other with haymaking and lifting the potatoes. This was one of Jacqueline's favourite times. 'When the tatties were ready to pick, there might be 30 or 40 folk – family and extended family and all the bairns – and we'd eat tattie soup for a week and go from one house to the next, helping each other out. It was so much fun!'

I'm here in July and in Shetland that's shearing time. Every farmer and crofter has an eye on the weather. Sheep need to be dry before they are relieved of their fleeces – not only are they easier and safer to handle, but if stored wet the fleeces will be worthless. The buzz of clippers and bleating of sheep reverberates from every shearing shed on the island. Days are long; the work is relentless and incredibly physical. So, when the job is done, the sheep back out on the hill, unnaturally white and looking like plush toys, and the fleeces rolled tight and stuffed into the big rectangular wool sacks awaiting sale, people gather to drink, eat and dance.

I'm not someone who relishes a party. I can't do crowds and don't wear clothes that make me feel uncomfortable. But a post-shearing party in a sheep shed on Shetland is a come-as-you-are, bring-the-whole-family affair. Tables are piled with plates of homemade food, drinks in paper cups. There's a bonfire in the yard sending sparks up into the darkening sky. Chatter and backslaps and guffaws of laughter. There are great-grannies and babes in arms, and all ages between, in Sunday best or jumpers and wellies, toe-tapping, jigging, then swirling to the irresistible, infectious call of the fiddle.

It is here I first meet Karen, Jacqueline and Willie's daughter, and she invites me to visit them a few days later. Tellingly, perhaps, she gives me directions to her parents' house rather than her own. 'I still spend quite a lot of time there,' she laughs, as if confessing something mildly shameful.

There's sunshine and no wind – a rare combination in Shetland – so when I drive down the single-track lane and descend towards the croft, everyone is outside. I'm greeted first by the enquiring noses and wagging tails of the farm's dogs, several generations of them, and then by three generations of Doulls. Karen introduces me to her father Willie, a quietly spoken man in his late sixties in well-worn jeans, shirt sleeves rolled-up. He has the tough, workmanlike hands of a farmer and eyes that smile. 'And this is my mum!' Jacqueline, dark-haired and smiling, is clearly the sort of person used to making anyone, stranger or not, feel instantly welcome. She gives me a warm hug.

'Come in! Come in!' she says. 'There's lunch – nothing much – but I thought you might be hungry. Mitchell! Ada!' she calls to her grandchildren, who are playing on the patch of grass at the side of the house. 'Lunchtime!'

I help carry plates piled with bread and cheese, salad and ham, cake and biscuits to the kitchen table, and we all gather around it, Willie at the head. Jacqueline pours tea and we help ourselves. It is a bright, modern room, uncluttered, with little evidence of the Doull family heirlooms amassed over the decades. No stuffed ducks on the dresser, although there are photos going back to when Willie was a young man; they show the croft smaller, with just a couple of low outbuildings alongside it. The landscape is unchanged, though, and I suspect if Willie's grandfather were able to see it now, it would feel as familiar as it always did.

I have always felt that the security and stability of my childhood, growing up in one place, gave me both the confidence and desire to leave it and live a more peripatetic life – perhaps because I subconsciously felt safe in the knowledge that I always had a home to go back to. I wonder if Karen felt the same as I did; whether her years growing up in the house that roots her family so firmly to this place gave her a restlessness. A desire to wander. She laughs. 'My husband Daniel and I built a house at the other end of Muckle Roe from where I grew up because that's where his family are from. It's only three miles from Mum and Dad's but I still feel homesick!'

She lived at home until she was 30, going away occasionally to see bands and to go to festivals. She knew she wanted to follow in her mother's footsteps and work with children, and she could do the training on Shetland. 'There was no need to waste the money going somewhere else to study when I could do it here.'

When she married Daniel, they both agreed they wanted to stay on Muckle Roe. 'There's nowhere else on Shetland I'd want to move to.' But there was a conundrum. Daniel wanted to live on the side of the island that he'd grown up on and Karen wanted to be close to her home patch. 'It was suggested we might live in the middle, but neither of us wanted to do that!' In the end, practicality made the decision for them. They were able to take on the vacant tenancy of a piece of land belonging to Daniel's father and got planning permission to build their house there. While they were building, they lived for part of the time with Daniel's family and part of it with Willie and Jacqueline. 'The thing is,' Karen muses, 'Mum and Dad's house is always such a busy house, there's always something happening. I would miss the commotion of being here when we moved into the new house at first. And I love the view here. I love looking out over the Sound. I just love it here.'

Their house is now finished and I wonder how someone who has such strong ties to the place in which they grew up goes about starting from scratch, trying to create a home somewhere different, albeit close by. 'When I chose the colours for the kitchen, I realised that subconsciously I'd chosen exactly the same colours of this kitchen. And I love old furniture and a traditional feel.

I wanted a farmhouse kitchen, for it to feel as homely as possible – and homely for me is here: is where I grew up.'

'And does it feel like home?'

Karen contemplates this question. 'We got married in the house, even though it wasn't quite finished, so it has a history now that we share. And Daniel did quite a lot of the building work so, again, that makes it feel that it really belongs to us. And it is in a beautiful spot with a beautiful view. And it feels even more like home since having the bairns.' She loves the fact that their children, Mitchell and Ada, are growing up literally in their family's footsteps. 'When I was growing up, I ran around the places that my dad played when he was a child, and now our children are running around in the places Daniel played, and probably his dad. There is something really nice about that. But this croft will really always be my home. I will always prefer it here.'

Willie gives his daughter a nod of assent from the opposite end of the table. For the last 20 years he has been a fencing contractor. 'And because of that, I know most of Shetland, including the bits you can't see from the road. I've done work on the Skerries and Papa Stour and as far north as Yell, but the only place I've seen on Shetland that I want to live is when I come over the top!' And everyone laughs because he is referring to the rise the lane climbs and descends before it makes its way down to his own front door.

Willie and Jacqueline rarely go on holiday. A couple of times, they went to stay overnight with Jacqueline's sister when her husband was the lighthouse keeper at Sumburgh, and later, on Bressay. They took a trip to the Western Isles of Scotland and go to Orkney and mainland Scotland, travelling once – unlikely as it sounds – to Glasgow, to see Dolly Parton. 'Although we were so far away from the stage,' Willie grunts, 'I'd have seen her better on the TV!' But travel holds very little appeal. 'The best bit about going on holiday,' Willie says decisively, 'is coming back home. I can go wherever I want, whenever I want. If I want peace and quiet, I can find it. And the people here: I could phone any of them at any hour of the day or night if I needed help and they would come. And they would ask the same of me. There is nobody you couldn't ask for help. So I feel relieved because when I'm away I don't really know where I am. Here I know everything.'

And now I understand why Willie seemed somewhat puzzled when I asked what home means to him. The Doulls are so rooted, so connected to this piece of land. It is as interwoven with generations of their history that it is as good as another member of the family. Which perhaps explains how it has never really crossed their minds to question why they feel so at home here. It is just so.

Badgers

———

We walk across the fields as the sun starts to appear over the hill, away to the left. An orange glow creeps towards us, returning colour to the monochrome pre-dawn landscape. It brings back the deep green of the grass, makes the dew that sits heavily on it, weighing down the blades, shimmer. It reaches the woods on the other side of the field, bringing definition back to the shadowy space, picking out the trunks of oak and beech, scattering gold highlights among the branches. A robin starts to trill in greeting.

Through the fields and down the track that will lead to the woods. The blackbirds start to sing now. The tiny, brown dart that is a wren bursts from the brambles, flits across my path, low to the ground. Disappears again. The world in waking. My feet leave the muddy gravel of the track for the soft squelch of leaves, following the way over a thick, mulchy carpet of browns. Here and there, the first optimistic shoots of spring are pushing up through the winter cover, stretching their green arms towards the light. I reach the copper beeches, bare of their deep, glossy, burgundy leaves now, although there are tight buds on the twiggy ends of the branches, and here I slow my pace, lightening my footsteps as I always do, conscious of the world beneath my feet.

The ground slopes gently up to my left. There's a small clearing behind the beech trees, one or two scattered holly bushes and brambles covering an area of humped and uneven earth. In places there are cave-like holes, entrances to low tunnels, the red clay soil at their mouths packed hard and worn smooth.

A badger sett is a maze of tunnels and chambers, excavated by the clan of animals that occupy it. Clans will often have small, outlying setts within their territories, but their main sett will be a large intricate labyrinth with a hundred metres or more of tunnels, branching off in all directions. Some will lead to other entrances – a sett can have as many as 40 different ways in and out – some to sleeping quarters, some to dead ends, all on different levels. The animals collect dried grass and leaves which they drag to the sett, often backwards in a comically ungainly fashion, to insulate the chambers where they sleep.

The sett is home to adult animals – both males and females – and their cubs. It will usually house six or eight badgers, but as many as thirty-five have been recorded living in one sett. And the sett will grow with the clan. New chambers may be dug for each successive brood of cubs and several generations will live together communally. Although outside the sett, badgers tend to feed and forage alone, inside, particularly when the weather is cold, the whole clan will snuggle up together to sleep in one chamber. And they all work together to maintain the sett, digging new tunnels and chambers, taking out the old bedding and bringing in fresh leaves and grass, although it tends to be the females that are the instigators of the housework. A study of a clan of badgers noted that when the female died and the male stayed on by himself, the sett started to look 'ill-kept and rather inactive . . .' It's not a case of the females being house proud. As well as ensuring the sett doesn't get infested with fleas and other unpleasant parasites they'd rather not share their space with, it needs to stay in good shape because clans pass their setts down to the next generation. The same family can live in a sett for decades. One was found to have been occupied by the same clan for over two centuries, a subterranean record of the family's history.

There is no sign of activity as I walk past the sett in the woods this morning, but still I tiptoe, not wanting to disturb a badger that may be sleeping beneath my feet.

no one leaves home until home is a sweaty voice in your ear
saying-
leave,
run away from me now
i don't know what i've become
but i know that anywhere
is safer than here

From 'Home' by Warsan Shire

Kindness

———

When you have no choice at all, when your fate is entirely in the hands of others, can the place you find yourself ending up in ever be home?

In 1989, a woman gave birth to her seventh child, a girl. She named her Jana. Jana grew up in the big house belonging to her father's family, surrounded by people who loved her. The house, in the Syrian city of Aleppo, was her world. Like the wider world beyond, it wasn't perfect. Her father died when she wasn't quite two years old, her older brother a couple of years later. Life was hard for her mother. Along with the grief she had to bear came money worries, and no one in the extended family was able to help much, struggling, as they were, to support their own children. But Jana's other brothers worked and so did her mother, and after a few years, things became easier. And it was, she says, wonderful to grow up part of a family which, when her brothers married and their wives came to live with them too, continued to grow.

The house was extended upwards. They added one floor, then another, creating the space for all three brothers to be able to live there with their own families. Although it was arranged as separate apartments, they did everything together. 'We ate together. At night, we sat together, we talked with each other. Here, when I see a young girl or a young boy who has left their family to go and live on their own, I can't understand how they live like that. It must be really hard.'

Jana pours thick, cardamom-scented coffee into small cups from a long-handled enamel pot, puts a plate of dates on the table, then sits down beside me on the sofa. Her husband, Abdul Karim, sits on the opposite sofa, legs drawn up to his chest. He's dressed for work and is watching something on his phone. On the wall above him is a painting, a monochrome image of pale grey flowers. There are house plants in the corner, green and lustrous and well-tended. There are more flowers in vases on the dining room table in the far corner and wall hangings depicting phrases from the Qur'an either side of the window overlooking the garden. The large television is tuned to an Arabic radio station. The music, the smell of the coffee, the warm courtesy with which I am greeted as I come in, removing my shoes to join the other pairs lined up in the hall, transport me. It is hard to believe that outside their front door there is not the hot, dusty bustle of a lively Syrian city, but a quiet cul-de-sac of newly built houses in a Welsh suburb, hunched under a leaden sky, rain falling with heavy, persistent monotony.

Jana was just 14 when she married Abdul Karim and, as is

customary, went to live in his family home. They weren't strangers, they'd lived nearby in the same neighbourhood, and Abdul Karim's mother was like a second mother to Jana. But still, she tells me, leaving her home, the only place she had ever known, was traumatic. 'I remember on my wedding day, when I was getting dressed and ready, I was crying, my mother was crying . . .' She took nothing with her other than her clothes and two vases her mother had given her as a wedding present.

It was a good marriage. Jana had grown up living hand to mouth. They had no savings – 'What we get, we spend.' Abdul Karim's family owned their own business, money was less tight, and Jana thought that having money would make her happy, that it would make her feel safe. 'But nothing makes you feel safer than when you are with your own family. Nothing makes you happier. It was Abdul Karim's family that made me happy.'

She gave birth to their first child just 10 months after they were married. She wasn't quite 15 years old. 'And when my daughter cried, I didn't understand why or what to do.' But Abdul Karim's mother lived upstairs and her own mother lived close by. 'That is why family is so important. I couldn't have managed without them.'

Their son was born two years later. Abdul was bright and talkative, but something wasn't quite right. He seemed to have trouble walking. 'I had a very, very nice neighbour; she is almost like another mother to me, and she tells me, "Jana, look at your son! He is not right. He is not walking right." And I say, "Maybe later, maybe later . . ." I didn't want to accept that something might be wrong. I couldn't understand why he was finding it hard to walk when everything else was fine. I thought, "He will learn. It will come."' But soon she had to accept that her son was struggling.

They spent all their money trying to find a doctor who understood what was wrong with Abdul. Each one they saw came up with a different diagnosis, but none was sure; none of them could offer any sort of treatment. Finally, after months of uncertainty and worry, of fruitless and expensive appointments, they found a doctor who recognised Abdul's symptoms. Tests confirmed his suspicions. Abdul had spinal muscular atrophy, an incurable condition that would require lifelong medical intervention and physiotherapy. No one could guess at a prognosis. Jana was heartbroken, desperate that there was nothing she could do to help her son get better. As ever, it was her family and her neighbours who gathered around her, told her they would always be there to help and support her.

What they didn't know – what no one could have predicted – was that in a few short years, Jana's family and her neighbourhood would be torn apart. The Syria where Jana had grown up was, she tells me, her eyes and voice soft and sad, a very nice country: 'There was no other country like Syria. It was the people who made the country. No one was very rich but no one was homeless. Everyone looked after each other. Families were strong. Communities were strong. And my city, Aleppo, was beautiful – very old with a big castle, many trees, a lovely park. Syria had everything. We were self-sufficient. We didn't need anything from the outside.'

But in March 2011, discontent started to bubble; there were murmured complaints against the government as prices for essentials like water and electricity became higher and higher. Criticism grew, fuelled by the perception that the government was getting rich on the deprivations of the people it was supposed to govern and protect. But speaking out in public was dangerous. Somehow, the police would get to hear of it and the offender taken away. 'And you couldn't say anything,' Jana tells me. 'You couldn't ask what would happen to them, where they were taking them, because if you did, they would arrest you too. We could only stand and watch.'

In other cities, people were beginning to take to the streets: peaceful protests that were met with disproportionate force. News was suppressed and at a time when few people had smartphones, information was slow to spread. But it did. Hamza Al-Khateeb, a 13-year-old boy, was arrested by police in the city of Daraa for shouting 'freedom' at them during a march. His body was returned to his family bearing terrible evidence of the most brutal and inhumane torture and mutilation imaginable. The story, when it got out, sparked a wave of horrified protest across Syria. In Aleppo, the government responded by sending police and soldiers and bombs into the streets.

That morning, Jana had gone with her two children to visit her mother while her husband was at work. One of her brothers had already left the city, taking his wife and family to the countryside to wait out this period of unrest. Abdul Karim joined his family in the afternoon and said they should leave too. They went to his family's house just outside the city. It had everything they would need for a short stay and they thought they wouldn't have to stay for long – a week at most until things settled down – so they took nothing with them. But it soon became apparent that the situation, far from settling down, was escalating – 'There were bombs everywhere. Houses were being destroyed. People were dying.' The family returned to Aleppo, but just to collect their clothes and take food from the freezer.

The house where they were staying was big, Jana says, with four bedrooms upstairs and a small kitchen, and downstairs a huge living room and another, much bigger kitchen. It had a garden, a swimming pool. They kept chickens and had fruit trees. More and more members of Abdul Karim's extended family started to arrive, fleeing a city where it was becoming too dangerous to stay. Jana remembers: 'There were about 45 people living there in the end. We made it work. The men lived downstairs and the women lived upstairs. It was summer, so people could sleep outside too. And we thought it would be fine because we might all be there for maybe ten days. Then two weeks. Then maybe one month.'

They stayed all summer. It wasn't easy, so many people living together, but having to occupy separate parts of the house. It was also getting harder to go out and to buy things. But at least they were safe from the bombs they could hear falling on their city, and there were no soldiers or police to harass them.

Aleppo was empty for the summer. Everyone left. But in the winter, they started to come back. The city was divided now:

some areas controlled by government forces and some by the rebels. It was a hard way to live but it was possible. Some of the shops re-opened. Abdul Karim went back to work while Jana stayed in their house with her children, but there was no electricity and most of the time there was no water either. And it was dangerous. 'One day a bomb fell very close to our house. Abdul was playing on the balcony. We weren't hurt and the house wasn't damaged, but all I could think was that he could have been killed. So I went back to the house in the countryside.'

A year into the war, Jana's mother and brothers returned to her childhood home in Aleppo and Jana would come into the city to visit them. The house was in an anti-government area and one winter's day a bomb fell on their street. It destroyed their neighbour's house – 'His son was killed. Other people were killed. We couldn't find their bodies. They were completely obliterated.' Jana's family home was damaged too and her brother was injured, although, mercifully, not seriously. But it was clear that they could no longer stay.

Two of Jana's brothers fled with their mother to Turkey, where an uncle was already living. For 18 months, Jana didn't see her mother. They had never been apart for so long. Even after Jana got married, she saw her mother almost every day. So she and Abdul Karim decided to go to Turkey to see her. Jana had never left Syria. She had no passport. The only way they could leave was illegally. She was also heavily pregnant with their third child.

Despite the risks, they left the house at 5am with the children, taking only two small bags and two loaves of bread, and travelled to the Turkish border. They joined a crowd of people hiding, watching the border guards, waiting for a moment when they could cross over. Abdul Karim and Jana were told they might have to wait an hour or two before the guards changed over, leaving the border unmanned just long enough, they hoped, to cross without being caught and shot. Jana was terribly, terribly frightened. Two teenage boys saw an opportunity to run. Some followed them, but Jana and Abdul Karim didn't think it was safe. They stayed in their hiding place and watched as the two boys were shot and killed by the border guards.

They waited for almost 12 hours before the chance came to make the terrifying dash to freedom. They made it across – Abdul in his father's arms, Jana holding their daughter's hand. They joined Jana's brothers and mother, and just days later, Jana gave birth to a baby girl. Abdul Karim got a job. Jana was back with her mother. It seemed like the start of a new life. Yet three months later, they returned to Syria.

'Why?' I ask, aghast. 'Why, when you risked everything to leave? Abdul Karim is working, and you have somewhere to live, and you're safe and with your mother. Why did you go back to Syria?'

'Because Abdul Karim's family is still there. And my things are there. And Abdul's doctor is there. And Turkey is too expensive. Abdul Karim's wages could only cover the rent, not pay for food.'

But on their return to Aleppo, they discovered that the children's school had closed and, worse still, Abdul's doctor had himself gone to Turkey. And there was no life, nothing they could do. Every day they would just wake up, clean the house, cook, eat and go back to sleep. The city was in ruins and it was dangerous. They had no choice but to return to Turkey. 'We didn't know how long we'd be there but we knew we couldn't come back to Syria until it was safe. But we said, one day, when the war is over, we will come back to our home.'

Even though they had stayed in Turkey before and had some family there, it was a difficult transition. Life for Jana became a seemingly endless onslaught of what at times seemed like insurmountable challenges. Gone was her support network of extended family and kind neighbours. Gone was the local knowledge that makes the everyday tasks routine. Gone was her ability to communicate. With three small children to look after, one with complex medical needs, she found herself on a never-ending trudge between government offices, hospitals and consulting rooms. They struggled with money. Abdul Karim's family were able to help a bit and Jana sold some of her jewellery so they could rent a house with some furniture. But the biggest hardship she had to overcome was the hostility she faced being unable to speak Turkish. She was shouted at, thrown out of doctors' offices and frequently reduced to tears of desperation. If they had enough money they paid for translators to come to the hospitals with her, but it was a luxury they could rarely afford.

She pours us more coffee, gathering herself, the stress and misery of those times still vivid in her memory. She settles back on the sofa and gives me a brave smile. 'It got better. After about two years, I could understand more of the language and communicate more easily, so I felt less helpless. I finally found a hospital who understood what was wrong with Abdul and could help us with him. We had a house. My mother was with me. Abdul Karim had work and I still had some jewellery to sell if we needed money. Life was getting easier.'

It was Abdul Karim who heard that the UN had set up a relief centre in one of the city's mosques, providing food, support and advice for refugees. 'But I didn't want to go. I told him, "I can't ask people for food. I can't ask for anything." ' But he persuaded her to try, and when an older Syrian lady she met told her how they had helped her and offered to come along with her, reluctantly Jana agreed. She went, pushing Abdul in a pram. He was too big to be in a pram now but he struggled to walk, and they had no other means for him to get around.

The UN worker she talked to asked her lots of questions, assessing her family's situation to ascertain what help they might need. Jana told the UN worker of the worries she had about Abdul, the struggles she still had to find proper care for him. 'And I knew, without it, I might lose him, and I was really scared.' They asked if she wanted to leave Turkey. Jana knew only too well the realities of trying to make a life in another new country, the hardships of taking on a new language, a new culture, a new set of challenges and uncertainties. It was a daunting, exhausting prospect. But, she says, 'I would go anywhere, to any country that could help my son.'

Her hope was that they would be sent to America because she believed they would get access to the best medical advice and expertise there. But America had closed its border to refugees from Muslim countries. She had a nephew in Germany, but Germany wasn't taking any more refugees at the time either. One of her sisters had settled in the UK, so it was decided that would be the best option. The UN made the application to the British government, and they waited.

In 2017, six months after the application was made, six years after the war in Syria had started, Jana, Abdul Karim and their children arrived in the UK. They were given temporary accommodation until a suitable house could be found for them, and Jana's sister was there offering the support and help Jana so desperately needed. As, once again, she was back to the misery and frustration of not being able to communicate, of being in a country where her looks and her clothes set her apart. They would stay, she thought, only as long as it took to stabilise Abdul's deteriorating health and until they had passports so that they could travel legally. Then, they would go back to Turkey. Even though she had been so unhappy there, at least, she reasoned, she had got through the worst and could manage to have some sort of life there. Here, in the UK, she had to start from nothing all over again.

'But this is before I knew what the people here were like; before I discovered they are really friendly,' Jana explains. 'When I cried, when I couldn't understand or make myself understood, people were kind. They would give me a hug. They would help me. Everyone helped us. There were doctors who could help my son. The school has done so much to help my children. I was given a teacher to help me learn English. We had financial help until my husband found a job. The government helped me make a life and a home here. I don't want to move again. I would feel like I've lost everything once more. I don't want to have to feel that again. And there is nothing now for me in Turkey. My lovely mother died about a year after we came here. I have my sister. That is important – to have someone who knows all about you, understands you. Knows about your life, knows your history. I go to college and I'm getting more confident with the language; I don't need help all the time. So, I'm OK now. I'm starting to enjoy life.'

'What about Syria?' I ask. 'Do you imagine ever returning to Syria?'

Jana's face clouds with the pain of memory. 'When you remember your city, how it was before, and when you see how it is now, I would say no. I'm scared to go there. I'm scared to see my home destroyed. Everything makes me scared. And my family is no longer there. It is not home anymore. We are different people and we have a different life now. There is no reason to go back. But I don't want my children to forget their culture. I don't want them to forget where they are from. And one day, if Syria recovers, I want to take them there. To show them the country that was my home.'

We hug goodbye. I walk through the rain to my car, struggling to process the conversation we have had, to comprehend how someone has enough courage and enough resilience to survive everything Jana has been through in her short life. Most of us have what I now realise is a luxury: some choice about where or how we live. Jana's life in Aleppo was centred around her extended family, her neighbours and her neighbourhood. Home was consistency; the reassurance, love and support of her mother and siblings; the familiarity and cohesion of her community. But when all that was blown apart, when everyone and everything she knew was gone, when she became stateless, rootless, was no longer a citizen, belonged nowhere, home was simply anywhere her family could be safe and her son could get treatment. Nothing else mattered.

Except that she discovered that there was one thing that did, the one thing that makes her feel at home now more than at any other time since she fled Syria.

Kindness.

The Man Who Fell from the Sky

—

The room is full of treasures. Glass-fronted cupboards against the walls and display cases in the middle, with just enough space to walk between them. There are wooden masks, wide-mouthed and blank-eyed. Intimidating. A little gruesome. Headdresses made from grass and feathers. Carvings in wood, dark with age. Woven baskets and fish traps. Spears. A quiver of arrows. Knives with ornate handles. Remnants of American military hardware: a battered metal munitions box, faded black letters stamped on khaki green. A bomb casing. The propeller of a plane. A wooden crate of empty glass Coca-Cola bottles. It's a private museum. A collection amassed over 30 years of exploring these islands, which belonged to someone who arrived here on the back of a story. And who became so enmeshed in the islands' history and culture that he never left. His home became here, and no longer there.

'Can you tell me about this photo?' I ask.

There are several photos on the wall, most of them portraits.

Women, with their hair cropped close to their heads, faces deeply lined, eyes dark wells of hidden thought. And younger girls, hands fluttering in front of nervously laughing mouths. Defiant men, bare-chested, muscles taut, standing proud and strong. A chief in full regalia. But the photograph I'm pointing to is different. Not a portrait, exactly, but an image with a tale to tell.

The photograph is black and white. It is of an elderly white man, lean and upright. His hair is grey and neatly cut, a little sparse, parted and combed. His short-sleeved shirt is untucked but crisp and uncreased. He appears tall but perhaps this is because he stands head and shoulders above the people crowding around him so tightly that there is no space visible between them, the lower half of his body swallowed up in the press of theirs. The faces of the crowd are all turned up towards the face of the white man, eyes fixed on him. Their ebony black skin gleams with a sheen of sweat in the intense light of a tropical sun. Every face is alight with joy. My own face is stretched into a smile the image has provoked. And that is even before I know the story.

The white man had been in the US Air Force during the Second World War and was one of the soldiers deployed to the Pacific to fight with the Australians against the Japanese. His plane was hit by Japanese fire. Although injured, he managed to get out and parachute down into the thick, mountainous jungle of an island below. Somehow, he had to find a way to survive and avoid capture by the Japanese on the ground.

The tropical jungles of the Pacific are hostile places. Thick with biting insects, venomous snakes, dangerous animals and vegetation that is often impenetrable. Alone, with no knowledge or experience of the terrain, chances of survival are slim. Yet the white man did survive. He lived in the forest for a month before he was found – not by the Japanese but by one of the tribes that inhabit the island, close to the coast. They too might have killed him but instead they took him to their village where for five months, they housed him, fed him, protected him and hid him from the Japanese until he was rescued.

After the war, the white man settled into domestic life in his hometown in America. He married and had children, but never forgot the people whose bravery and generosity saved his life. Every year, he sent money to the village via the local mission and the day he retired he did what he had always promised himself he would do: he returned to live with the people who had made their home his.

The Hippos of Colombia

When notorious Colombian drug lord Pablo Escobar was shot
by police in 1993, he was the richest, most infamous, person in
the world. His cocaine empire had amassed him a fortune of
$30 billion and worldwide notoriety.

In common with many humans who have made astonishing
amounts of money, Escobar indulged in rampant and showy
consumerism, just in case anyone missed the fact that he had
done well for himself. His homes abroad included a mansion in
Miami Beach (pink) and not just one island, but an entire
archipelago in the Caribbean. His Colombian abode was
Hacienda Nápoles, a vast estate comprising various hallmarks of
the super-rich – a private airport, a Formula 1 racing track, a
brothel. It housed his collections of vintage and luxury cars, art
and sculpture, but he also had a penchant for collecting exotic
animals.

Given that Colombia is second only to Brazil when it comes to
biodiversity, why Escobar felt the need to collect animals from

elsewhere on the planet is anybody's guess, and I don't suppose anyone dared to question it. And if you can smuggle enough cocaine to make you $30 billion, smuggling elephants, rhinos, giraffes and zebras into your garden is presumably a breeze. His private zoo was rumoured to have over 200 animals, including 3 female hippos and one – as it turns out – very virile male.

After Escobar's death, most of the animals in his collection were re-homed in other, more orthodox collections throughout the world, but not the hippos. Herbivores they may be, but they are infamously territorial, have big teeth and very powerful jaws, and are responsible for more human deaths in Africa than any other mammal. So, it seems even people accustomed to dealing with the world's most ruthless drug lord were not prepared to take on his hippos.

The hippos, thanks to that one enthusiastic male, have multiplied. There are now estimated to be over 130 of them. Colombia may not have hippos among its vast array of native species, but it can provide everything a hippo needs to survive, which is not much: a body of water large enough to submerge in and grass to graze. There is a mixed reaction to them. Some people love them; others worry that as an invasive species, they will upset the local ecosystem as well as posing a danger to humans living and working along the same water courses. But as vet Gina Paola Serna points out, they shouldn't be demonised, nor seen as Escobar's legacy. 'They are simply animals that escaped and bred and made a home in an environment that is not their own.'

Carpets and Curtains

———

'I keep feeling like I've got to feather the perfect nest, but what that "perfect" is, I'm not sure. I've got three daughters. The eldest has gone to uni this year. She's 19. The youngest is 14. And I'm having a midlife crisis. Well, a beyond-midlife crisis, as I'm 51. I'm thinking, "Why am I constantly moving on to the next thing?" Because time is running out. My girls have nearly left home and then there won't be a family home anymore. I haven't settled down. I am always looking for whatever the answer might be, but I've never quite found what I thought I was looking for.'

Mel and I sit at her kitchen table nursing cups of coffee. There's a pan of homemade soup on the range and the smell of warm bread. A dog lies in a state of sleepy bliss in a basket and a cat climbs in through a window, weaves its sinewy way to a patch of sunshine on the sill and stretches luxuriously out. There is a jug of garden flowers on the dresser, a scented candle flickering. The tastefully muted colours of the walls and woodwork contrast with bright artwork and cheerful fabrics. It is an idealised vision of home, one an art director might dream up for a Richard Curtis film, but it doesn't feel contrived. Instead, it feels welcoming, an easy place to sit and chat, even though the woman I am chatting to is someone I don't know at all. We have only just met, and this is not her home.

Just a few weeks ago Mel, her husband Andy and their daughters had been living in a grade I-listed manor house with three and a half acres of formal gardens. Morville Hall was bequeathed to the National Trust in the 1960s and had always been rented out to private tenants. In 2019, the National Trust was looking for new tenants to take it on and Mel and Andy, more on a whim than anything else, went to see it. It was a quest for adventure. A quest to break with the norm.

'I was the nerdy girl at school. The bespectacled, frizzy-haired, clever one. And I think what happened when I was growing up made me believe that I should follow a very conventional path – go to university, aspire to a well-paid, sensible career. I felt that was expected of me and that I had little choice to do otherwise.'

It's not hard to imagine that a childhood like Mel's would engender a need for security, for normality. Her formative years were overshadowed by her parents' faltering relationship and a lack of money. Her father was involved in the very early days of computer programming, a job that involved moving his family almost constantly, leaving a house they had been in for just a year to live in Germany when Mel, the eldest, was eight. The German house is the first house Mel really remembers, partly because it was a new build that had never been lived in by anyone else. 'We started from scratch. We had to get all our furniture from this store called Ikea, which no one in the UK had heard of back then. So it was rather weird, being surrounded by brand new things that didn't really feel part of us. But I suppose in the end it felt like home because it was all we knew.'

Three years later, they were back in the UK and their father bought an old farmhouse in the north-west of England for them to live in. It was falling to bits. Enormous and ramshackle and 'full of huge spiders' recalls Mel, with a visible shudder. Her abiding memory of that time is of her mother gamely wallpapering and painting, on a constant quest to make the house more attractive and homely, but her efforts were in vain. It was big and cold; the modern flat pack furniture they'd bought from Germany was ill-fitting and at odds with its outdated surroundings. There was no money for proper carpets, so mismatched scraps covered some bits of the floor. There were no curtains.

Her father, obsessed with his work, with trying to develop a new software system that would rival Microsoft, was barely at home; he never helped try to improve the neglected house or tend the gardens. Mel took refuge in her bedroom, the only place in the house she could find solace. There she studied, her goal to get to a top university, which she felt was what everyone expected of her and would maybe, somehow, fix the situation the family was in. Because things were becoming increasingly fraught. Eventually her father's enterprise crashed, leaving the family's paltry finances in tatters. He took to the bottle and then, one day, just upped and left for good.

Mel's mother and siblings stayed on in the old farmhouse while Mel went to university. But during her first year, her father contacted his family to say he could no longer pay the mortgage on the house, so he'd rented it out to students, who were due to arrive the following week. They had to leave so quickly, Mel said, that they had no time to find anywhere to go. There was no chance for her to even pack up her things, which were just shoved up in the attic and eventually ransacked or stolen by the tenants. 'It was all so quick, I never had a chance to say goodbye to that house. In one fell swoop I lost my home. I lost my dad. I lost everything we'd been used to.'

Respite came from her academic life. She had dutifully followed the path she felt had been laid out for her: she was at Bristol University and studying economics, a route that would ensure she was always in work and financially secure. It was there she met Andy, who, having been given every encouragement and chance by his adopted parents to make a success of his life, was reading law. 'So, we were on track for the life we both felt we'd been channelled towards. I was going to be an accountant, he was going to be a lawyer, we were going to make loads of money and everything was going to be fine!'

But something didn't sit comfortably with either of them. They didn't quite fit in with the crowd that surrounded them: young men and women from more privileged backgrounds, whose drive for success was more about status and material possessions than Andy and Mel's more prosaic need for security and stability. And both of them had a yearning to rebel, just a bit; to veer off the track that would have had them follow their university peers into city jobs and comfortable houses in south-west London. They took the city jobs but when it came to where they wanted to make home, they went rogue. It was a statement, proof to themselves and to anyone they knew that they had their own minds, could make their own choices, did not need to follow the herd. So they bought a flat in Rotherhithe. 'It was like a ghost town back then,' Mel tells me, refilling our coffee mugs. 'There was absolutely nobody like us there at all. But we loved it. We absolutely loved it. It had history. It had character. It was different, and that made it exciting.'

They set about creating the home neither of them felt they had ever had. And they started from scratch. Andy had his books, while Mel had barely anything from her childhood at all, apart from the recollections of living in a place with no carpet or curtains because they couldn't afford them.

'Rag-rolling was a thing, then,' Mel says, with a slight grimace.

'It was!' I laugh. 'I rag-rolled the kitchen of our first house. Terracotta. It looked awful but I was so proud of it!'

'We went terracotta too,' laughs Mel. 'It must have been *the* colour of the early nineties. We spent weeks rag-rolling almost every room, and they were huge rooms, looking out over the river. And then, because I was earning a good salary, I went and spent a small fortune on having really beautiful curtains made, and on, what was, for me, the absolute height of decadence – we had carpets fitted everywhere. They were the things I knew would make our flat feel cosy and consequently more homely in the way the house I grew up in never did. They are the creature comforts that you take for granted unless you haven't had them.'

But conformity caught up with Andy and Mel in the end. The birth of their first daughter prompted a move from London to the suburbs of Surrey, near Andy's parents. They lived there for 15 years, moving just once in that time. 'And they were proper family houses,' Mel says. 'We had the playroom, we had the garden. We ticked the boxes. And they did feel like home, particularly with our girls being there. But even though they were cosy and comfy, they had the curtains and the carpets, and our children were happy, both Andy and I still felt a niggling sense that the life we were living and the trajectory we were on was not really us. There was still something missing.'

After Andy's parents died, there seemed no compelling reason for them to stay in Surrey and both of them felt the urge to change everything – not just where they lived, but how they lived. Andy wanted to go back to university and study ancient history, Mel to explore her artistic side that duty and practicality had never given space to before. They settled on Shropshire. It wasn't an entirely random decision. Although neither of them had any connection with the county, they knew no one there or really anything about it, geographically it wasn't too far from Mel's family. Although she had lost all contact with her father, her mother and two siblings were still living near to where Mel had grown up in Cheshire.

'Our friends thought we were mad. They just didn't understand. They kept saying, "Why would you do that? Why would you give up everything you've got?"' And Mel couldn't really explain it, to her friends or even to herself. She just felt that there was somewhere out there where she belonged and she was determined to find it. There would be the dream house in the dream village if they just looked hard enough. So that's what they did; Andy at the wheel, Mel with a map of Shropshire on her knees. But nowhere felt right. There was no dream village with the perfect house.

Mel began to feel panicky and started to lose the courage of her convictions, wondering whether, instead of taking the leap and buying something, they play it safe and rent. See if they like it. And that's when they found the details for Morville Hall. 'It looked too good to be true. It was absolutely beautiful!' Mel laughs at the memory. 'Andy was dead set against even entertaining the idea, but for me, it offered the possibility of adventure, of making life seem a bit more exciting again.' And it was in a part of Shropshire they hadn't explored, further south, where the landscape is hillier and, in Mel's view, prettier.

They made an appointment to see the house and Mel remembers that her legs were shaking as they approached it; she felt genuinely anxious at the thought of living somewhere as daunting as that. The outgoing tenant was a well-known interior designer and the whole place looked, in Mel's words, like something from a magazine. And the scale of it was overwhelming. The hall alone was over 60 metres square. It led onto three massive reception rooms and a vast kitchen, all with enormously high ceilings, behind which were lots of smaller back rooms. Upstairs, there were seven bedrooms, two dressing rooms and two rather old-fashioned and rudimentary bathrooms. Their first reaction was 'How ridiculous! Can you imagine having a place like this as your home?'. But then, as they walked around, Mel started to feel differently. She started to feel excited by the challenge of taking it on.

The National Trust ask to interview any prospective tenants of properties on the scale of Morville Hall and make it very clear that living in a large historic house is not straightforward and requires a lot of hard work and dedication. Mel, with her accountant's head on, looked over the spreadsheets they were shown, weighed up the costs and concluded that they could live there with the same outgoings that they already had. They went back to look at the house again and stood in the garden, looking at each other, both asking 'Shall we?' It was at that moment the National Trust rang them and offered them a five-year lease starting in May. It was January.

The first challenge was how to furnish it. The previous tenants had owned all the furniture, rugs and curtains, and were taking everything with them. The furniture Mel and Andy already owned would be nowhere near enough for even a couple of rooms. 'It was like trying to furnish a doll's house, but on a vastly different scale,' Mel said. They went to auctions, buying up all the biggest pieces of furniture they could find, often for a song, because no one else had the space for them. 'We found a huge oak cupboard which takes five people to carry and is beautiful. We got it for £20.'

They moved into the house in July. Andy had enrolled at university in Birmingham and their daughters had places at a local school. Mel threw herself into the full-time job of looking after the house. And it really was a full-time job. In its heyday, the house had employed ten servants; now there was just Mel. But she loved it, particularly the garden, where she spent hours digging and weeding and planting, although she concedes that they hadn't really appreciated just how much they were taking on. But still, it was exciting, it was different, it was contrary. It seemed, finally, to be the thing Mel had been looking for ever since her father took away their family home. 'It had a magical quality to it that I can't quite really put into words. We found something there that we had never been able to find before. We'd come off the treadmill, left the rat race behind and slowed right down. We no longer felt the pressure to conform, to be what in other people's eyes is successful. We felt calm and at ease. It was crazy that a house like that could make us feel that way. It was bloody hard work living there. It wasn't warm – even in summer and in winter it was absolutely freezing – and it wasn't cosy, but I just loved it.

Within the first few months, she and Andy were already talking about extending the lease to ten years, dreaming about their daughters getting married in the gardens. When lockdown struck and Andy and their daughters were all studying at home, the house came into its own. Their lives and their whole existence revolved around it. It became their world. And it made them realise the importance of family, familiarity and peace. Even though, at the back of Mel's mind, she knew the house would never belong to them, the very intense way they ended up living there during the pandemic made it feel absolutely part of them, made it intrinsic to the fabric of their family. Mel's search for that unquantifiable something was over. 'It was a fairy-tale dream,' she says, staring into her cup.

That fairy-tale dream was swept away in a torrent of dark, treacle-brown water that burst through the sixteenth-century ceiling of their kitchen one morning, nearly two years into their five-year lease. A water tank in the attic had catastrophically failed. The kitchen and dining room had to be fenced off from the rest of the house. Scaffolding was erected. Industrial fans and dehumidifiers ran 24 hours a day. 'We felt so displaced. I know it sounds ridiculous because it is such a big house, but rooms have a function. Your kitchen is your kitchen. Your dining room is your dining room. But we had to move everything into other rooms. Everything felt chaotic and out of control and the noise from the fans was unbearable.'

I wonder why they didn't move out, but they couldn't. It was the middle of the pandemic. There was nowhere for them to go. But for Mel, it was more than that. Even though the house didn't belong to them, even though they had lived there for less than two years, they felt protective of it, felt that it had been let down, should have been looked after better. That it never should have been allowed to go for so many decades without fundamental repairs. To leave it would have been to abandon it and she couldn't bear the thought of that. So they camped in the rest of the house while work went on to try to repair the damage.

It was eight months before the ceiling was patched up and the scaffolding removed. The ceiling remained stained and brown, and damp bloomed on the walls, but they could finally move their table back in and their kitchen became their kitchen again. 'I was so happy, I can't tell you!' But it was clear the house had reached a critical stage, that further investigation and salvage works needed to be done to preserve it. Andy and Mel agreed to move out when their five-year lease was up in two years' time. And as soon as that decision was made, knowing that their life there had no future, all the fun they had had seemed to dissipate. 'It spoiled everything and changed everything forever.'

The house seemed to give up with them. Another water tank failed causing a second flood; the boiler was condemned; a plague of moths destroyed clothes and wall hangings; jackdaws launched an invasion down the chimney. In the end, when the temperature in their bedroom was just 11 degrees and no number of blankets or clothing could keep them warm, they had to concede that the house was barely habitable and neither it, nor they, could last another two years. 'I feel so bereft now because I have never before felt that level of emotional involvement in a house, even though we only lived there for three years. I cried and cried when we left. It broke my heart.'

Their adventure was over.

Mel ladles soup into bowls and cuts generous slices of bread.

'I made the butter!' she says, with justifiable pride. 'Just whizzed up cream in a food processor until it separated.'

'I can't believe you've only been here a few weeks,' I say truthfully, because there is no hint that they've just moved in, no sign of boxes or piles of stuff that hasn't yet found its place. Nor does it feel like the temporary stopgap Mel tells me it is. For someone who grew up in the most unhomely of homes, this house is evidence, despite her claims to the contrary, that Mel has developed a strong sense of what she needs around her to make a place comfortable and somewhere she is happy to be. I assume, too, that it is something of a relief, after all the emotional and physical upheaval of the last few months, that it is good to be somewhere more straightforward. But Mel shakes her head. She would do it all again. She loved the adventure. Loved the unconventionality of the way of life. Pondering why she felt so distraught when they left, she says, haltingly at first, 'I suppose home normally is your safe, boring place, isn't it? Where you go and put your feet up and nothing really changes?' Then, surer of herself: 'I think, weirdly, because we had so much change and upheaval, it made the house feel even more of a home. It brought the whole family together and made it fun and exciting.'

There are other things, too, living in Morville Hall taught her in her quest for home. She loves living in a rural area, being outside beyond the confines of a garden, being able to walk in the hills. So this corner of Shropshire, which they discovered by chance, is where they want to stay. They like having neighbours, being part of a community, being near friends. 'I wouldn't want to live in something so big again,' she says, definitely. 'There simply weren't enough hours in the day to keep it clean, so I always felt a little bit defeated. And whatever anyone says, those creature comforts, when you know what life is like without them, are incredibly important. My home has to have carpet. And curtains. And heat. But I still want it to be an adventure.'

I went into a house, and it wasn't a house,
It has big steps and a great big hall;
But it hasn't got a garden,
A garden,
A garden,
It isn't like a house at all.

I went into a house, and it wasn't a house,
It has a big garden and great high wall;
But it hasn't got a may-tree,
A may-tree,
A may-tree,
It isn't like a house at all.

I went into a house, and it wasn't a house -
Slow white petals from the may-tree fall;
But it hasn't got a blackbird,
A blackbird,
A blackbird,
It isn't like a house at all.

I went into a house, and I thought it was a house,
I could hear from the may-tree the blackbird call . . .
But nobody listened to it,
Nobody
Liked it,
Nobody wanted it at all.

'The Wrong House' by A A Milne

The Second House

———

I still feel guilty about that house. About what we did to it. The arrogance with which we went in and walked around its rooms. The excitement we felt about its 'potential', seeing only what we thought we could turn it into instead of what it was. Which was a home. And perhaps that was where we went wrong. It wasn't the initial choice we made. It was the subsequent ones.

We had stayed on in our first house for another four years after our return from Africa. I was restless and unhappy for many months, overwhelmed by the feeling of hopelessness that comes with searching for something you can't find. And I knew that however hard I tried it was in vain, because what I was looking for wasn't here. It was back there. Or that is what I believed. It was, I suppose, a sort of homesickness, if you are allowed to sicken for somewhere that is not your home. To feel the hollow pit of yearning for something intangible and invisible. Because it wasn't a building I hankered for – we hadn't lived in one for any length of time while in Africa. Nor was I particularly sorry to see the back of the Ford Cortina, although I had, and still have, very fond memories of it, despite its errant ways. It was something else I missed that I couldn't quite pinpoint, but it seemed to have something to do with a sense of belonging. Because I had felt that I had belonged there, in those big, wild spaces, in the dust and the heat, exposed to the elements. Part of nature. More than I ever felt I belonged in the capital city of my home country.

I was distracted, in the end, by work. I had struggled to find a job when we got back, not helped, I'm sure, by my aura of negativity, which only got worse after every rejection. But eventually, someone was brave enough to offer me a job which was both demanding and fascinating, and, better still, involved being out of London a lot of the time. That short contract led to another and another – each one challenging, each one involving travelling to other parts of the country and, increasingly frequently, abroad. Working overseas, I was to discover, is not remotely like being on holiday, whatever anyone thinks. But it brought back the unpredictability and the lack of a fixed routine that I had so loved about our life on the road.

I had swum free of the doldrums but hadn't quite banished the niggling urge to make a more fundamental change to our lives and move house. Instead of just glancing at the posters in estate agents' windows, we started to pause long enough to scan the prices and read the details of the ones we thought we might be able to afford. Then came the day when we pushed open the door and sat side by side on chrome-armed chairs, giving our details to a young, effervescent salesperson, who promised us that finding *exactly what we were looking for* was what they excelled at.

I can't remember now what we imagined we were looking for. We wanted to move to a slightly different area to meet prosaic requirements, like being closer to public transport and nearer shops. And I know we wanted an outside space that was more of a garden than a cramped, concrete yard. But otherwise, I don't think we had very fixed ideas, being of the belief that we'd know it was right when we saw it.

Of course, if we were going to do this, we had to sell our house first. I remember the pang I felt when I came home to see the For Sale sign erected by the front gate. The tiniest twinge of doubt. But it was exciting. We were throwing our lives up into the air and seeing where they would land.

'You said you didn't mind considering a house that needed a bit of work?' said the voice on the other end of the phone. 'A house has just come up in the right area but it needs a bit of a refurb. There's an open viewing on Saturday. It's the only way we can do it as the gentleman who lives there isn't on the phone.'

We joined a small knot of people on the pavement outside the terrace of red brick houses, taller and more substantial than our railway worker's cottage. The lime trees planted at intervals along the side of the road gave a sense of – perhaps grandeur is too grand a word – but an aspiration of something like it. Any grand ideas we might have had while outside quickly disappeared when we all trooped through the front door. Couples looked at each other askance, trying to hide their shock that someone could actually live in conditions like this. The floorboards in the narrow hall were bare and, in places, rotted through. The banisters up the uncarpeted stairs were missing spindles. The ceiling in the empty back bedroom had partially collapsed. Huge cracks zigzagged across the walls like livid scars. There was an old wooden single bed and a wardrobe in another room, but nothing else. No carpet, no other furniture. The bathroom didn't look like it had been updated – or indeed used – since the house was first built in the 1860s.

The other people were already leaving, daunted by the sheer scale of what needed to be done, but I became more and more excited with every room we went into, ignoring the cracked Bakelite switches falling off the walls, exposed wiring, gloomy front room and a kitchen that was just a narrow galley, with a stained butler's sink set into a waterlogged wooden draining board resting on a couple of cupboards, one with a missing door. A dank side return, running between the neighbour's garden fence and the wall of the kitchen, led into a patch of waste ground – broken slabs and waist-high nettles. I stood in the middle of it and looked at Ludo. 'It's perfect!'

There was no need for a survey. It was obvious, even to the inexpert, that the house had to be gutted. And that was its appeal. We could make it wonderful. Mould it to be exactly as we wanted it. It would be bespoke. Our ideal home. We made an offer on the spot and it was accepted. Then came the flurry of finding the people who could help us make this transformation. We were advised we should have an architect. A friend had a friend . . . We met him and showed him around the house before the sale was complete, taking a punt. We talked about the things we wanted – the big, open-plan, eat-in kitchen, knocking down walls to create a light, bright sitting room, lined with bookshelves. Changing the layout upstairs to make another bathroom. Incorporating lots of built-in cupboards and clever storage to maximise the narrow space and not clutter it up with too much furniture. We envisaged the visual impact of walking into what, from the outside, looked like a bog standard Victorian terraced house, but was in fact a space that exemplified the contemporary: clean lines, sleek plastered walls, stripped oak floors, internal glass, shadow gaps (we weren't sure what they were but the architect assured us we would want them) and carefully hidden appliances. Everything painted white. Builders came to quote, with much teeth-sucking and rolling of eyes and the occasional muttered, 'Christ, you must be mad.'

What was obvious from the start was that we were not going to able to live there for some time. A kind friend offered his garage to store our stuff, a spare room to sleep in and the rest of his house to share. His offer not only went beyond generosity; it made the whole undertaking possible. Because not only was the house we were buying uninhabitable, it was going to be very expensive to rectify. To be able to live rent-free and devote every moment we had to earning money to pay for the work it required was the only way we were ever going to pull this off.

Anyone who has ever undertaken any sort of renovation of a house knows that it takes twice as long and costs three times more than even the most pessimistic of estimates. And so it was. Months into the process, we would go round to see how things were going, imagining how it would have taken shape, only to find the roof was still off, the foundations exposed, acrow props and ladders and piles of rubble everywhere. The air thick with dust and no hint that anything had moved on at all.

A year in, our kind host himself moved house. We hauled our stuff out of his garage and into a storage unit. We went to housesit for another friend who was away for a month, but then stayed on once he came back, getting increasingly desperate and increasingly tired of living out of a duffle bag. This was a different kind of transience from the one we had embraced and so enjoyed in Africa. There we felt in control of our destiny, whereas here we were utterly dependent on so many things over which we had no control. The stress came not just from trying to meet the burgeoning costs of the building, and the worry that we had long since outstayed our welcome at our friend's flat, but also from the fact that we were, to all intents and purposes, homeless. We had no retreat. Nowhere to escape to. No space that had our things in it. Those familiar comforts – the books, the pictures, our own clutter in the bathroom. I had no idea I would ever feel this way. I was free-spirited. Happy to go anywhere, anytime. I was as good as nomadic. But as I was to discover – way into the future – true nomads are just as tethered as we house dwellers are. They have just as strong a sense of where they belong. And at that moment, this was what we were missing. We didn't belong anywhere.

In desperation, we moved in before the work was completely finished, camping in the rooms that were more-or-less done, our furniture and belongings piled up and still in boxes until we could start unpacking. I don't remember any feeling of excitement on the day we moved in. More a feeling of resignation, that we were moving there under duress, imposed on ourselves by the guilt we felt towards our host and the impatient belief that, if we moved in, the work would go quicker. .

Finally, when we waved the builders off for the last time, could unpack the boxes, hang pictures, arrange books on shelves, put our clothes in the wardrobes and push bits of furniture around until they were in the right place; when, at last, we had a space that was ours, designed and built and decorated to our spec, with our things in, where we could shut the door and just be, did we feel euphoric? No. No, we didn't. Well, I didn't. I felt, instead, the crush of anti-climax.

I looked around at a house unrecognisable from the one we had first seen. No longer did it have its air of destitution and dereliction. No longer did we fear a foot falling through a rotten stair, being electrocuted when we turned on a light or concussed by the sudden collapse of a ceiling. But no longer did it feel like a home. Because it had been a home to someone for a very long time. An old man had lived in this house for 40 years with his brother, and whatever the rest of us thought, when we were walking around on the day of the viewing, was immaterial. This house was his home. And by sweeping away his history so entirely, removing it altogether, we also managed to remove any sense of that building being a home. And unlike when we had bought our first house, when the changes we made we did ourselves – the painting, installing the kitchen – here we'd done nothing, other than hand everything we'd earned over to the people who did the work for us. So, not only had we obliterated the old story that made this house a home, we hadn't done anything to create our own. And now it was a blank canvas that we didn't know how to paint. It wasn't home. And I knew, almost instantly, that it never could be.

Birds and Flowers

———

I've been in Shetland for a week and, although it is mid-July, and England and Wales are wilting in the oppressive temperatures of an unprecedented heatwave, this is the first day it has been warm enough to sit outside here, albeit in a jumper. 'We've not had much of a summer,' the islanders tell me apologetically. And my first days here were unseasonably windy, as well as wet and cold. But I've been to these islands several times before. The weather can change in the blink of an eye, can vary from island to island – indeed, from bay to bay. The islands' wayward and unpredictable nature is, I think, the root of their charm. There is still a wildness here, a sense their human inhabitants are not in charge but live at the hand of more powerful forces.

My previous visits have all been for work – days scheduled and timetabled, nights in hotels. But this time is different. I'm staying at my friend Jon's croft on the island of Whalsay, looking after things while he is working away, an opportunity I leaped at. Despite the weather, I've grown to love these islands, with their stark, treeless beauty, strong communities and unaffected authenticity. My duties are light. There are cats and hens to feed, eggs to collect and sheep to keep an eye on, but otherwise, my days are my own. I buy food at the island's two shops, cook, peg out the washing, read, walk. The house sits on a low ridge at the north end of the island. An ever-changing seascape surrounds it on three sides: neighbouring islands appear and disappear from view, gannets dive, boats churn through the water and whales glide. Beyond here are just a couple more cottages, a loch and, incongruously, a golf course – 'The Northernmost Golf Course in the UK' according to the sign on the club house wall.

I'm not a golfer and usually abhor the sterility and close-cropped uniformity stamped onto a landscape to create a course, but this one is different. Sheep graze the fairways and bask on the greens. There has been no need to create hazards because they already exist. The course weaves between rock outcrops, burns, hollows and ponds and is surrounded on three sides by cliffs – some low, some tens of metres high – that rise out of the sea below. Oystercatchers harangue the players, starlings swoop and chatter, gulls shriek, ravens cronk, grey seals raise their heads from the water and observe from offshore. The ground between the fairways is peaty heathland, uneven under foot, a patchwork of bog and drier land, carpeted in grasses and flowers. There are swathes of fluffy bog cotton and purple heathers; tiny, vibrantly yellow rock roses; clover, willowherb and sheep's-bit. Twite and wheatear, birds that relish these coastal moors, flit among the rocks and foliage, and Shetland bees – large, fluffy ginger and yellow bumbles – forage and feast.

Summer days here are long and already I've established a daily routine. I wake early and this morning there are rays of sunlight forcing their way between the curtains. The sky is delicate blue, with almost no clouds. I look down on the low trees and shrubs that Jon – against all odds – has managed to grow and sustain in this fearsomely windy place. They are barely moving; the leaves of the willows and blossoms on the dog roses ripple in a tickling breeze. The sea, which until today has been choppy and grey, is flat, metallic, burnished silver. I feed the animals and, daring to leave my coat behind, walk out to greet the day with the curlews, whimbrels and terns. I exchange morning pleasantries and relieved comments on the improving weather with a man moving his sheep and an old couple out in their garden. The island dialect is strong and lilting but they make kind allowances for the outsider. I wave, as is the custom, to the driver of a passing car.

I return to the croft, make a mug of tea and sit on a bench, leaning against the stone wall of the house and looking out to sea. It is infinitely peaceful. I feel very content, very comfortable, very happy to be here. A butterfly has also been brought out by the sun and I watch it fluttering between the foxgloves, landing briefly to bask, opening its creamy black-tipped wings to absorb the warmth. It is a cabbage white, not native to these islands. Its caterpillars are thought to have been transported here in crates of cabbages grown in the more temperate south and delivered by the NAAFI to feed the troops stationed on the islands during the

Second World War. It seems hard to imagine that even if the caterpillars managed to develop into butterflies, they would survive the tough and unfamiliar environment they found themselves in. But they not only survived, they made Shetland home and are now the islands' only resident butterfly. There's something of a parallel, I think, between the butterfly on the foxgloves and the man who planted them.

Jon moved to Shetland in the autumn of 2003, having bought his house off the internet, sight unseen, earlier that year. This apparently rash decision, to up sticks from Kent and move pretty much as far away as he could while still remaining in the UK, was, in Jon's mind, entirely rational: a response to a lonely, rather unhappy and unsettled childhood in the Somerset Levels and Dorset's Blackmore Vale.

As a family, they moved every four or five years because of his father's work. 'I lived with a permanent sense of transience and impermanence. I was sent to a horrible boarding school.' His voice shudders at the memory. 'It was a very desensitising experience – I craved a family and a feeling of home being permanent.' Respite of sorts came through the books of Gerald Durrell and the discovery of the natural world. Inspired by Durrell, he too would bring back animals and hide them in his bedroom – 'I kept slow worms under my bed . . .' But the place he was happiest was with his grandmother in Cornwall. She lived in an old mining town, not somewhere that attracted the tourists and second-homers, but where, Jon recalled, the sense of community was still really strong – a result perhaps, of the constancy that comes from people living there, not just all year round, but for years, for generations.

Jon went to university in Kent and afterwards stayed there, moving into a semi-detached house in a small village. But after a few years, he started to look at the world around him and to question whether this was the way he wanted to live and work for the rest of his life. And he knew it wasn't, that the south-east of England was not where he wanted to be. He craved space but also the feeling of belonging that comes from being part of a community. His first inclination was to go to Cornwall, the only place where, growing up, he had felt at home. 'But I realised there was no work, apart from seasonal work – nothing that was going to enable me to make a living – and to get the sort of rural place I wanted was out of my price range.'

That is when his thoughts turned to Shetland. He had been visiting the islands every year since 1992. His early interest in wildlife had never diminished and his first trip, to go bird watching for a week on Fair Isle, was followed by a two-week trip the next year, until he found himself returning every year, for longer and longer, and during different seasons. 'The wildlife on Shetland is insanely good!' he explained. 'But I also realised there was the same feeling I got when I stayed with my grandmother as a child – the feeling of everybody looking out for each other. I felt like I'd stepped back into something that felt pleasing and familiar. I loved it! But this wasn't a holiday romance. I'd seen

Shetland looking wonderful and I'd seen her when she was really, really bad. And even then, I still liked the place.'

In the decade he had been visiting, he'd got to know the islands well enough to have a very strong idea of where he did and didn't want to live, dictated by two principal factors, work and wildlife, with wildlife top of the list – 'I realise it is not the usual house-moving set of criteria . . .' So Jon set his sights on being on the east side of Shetland rather than the west. 'The west is lovely – I love it – but the east side gets more migrant birds. And much as the islands of Unst and Fetlar are wonderful, I didn't want to live on either of them because I knew I'd have a job, probably in Lerwick as that's the main town, and I didn't want a commute of two ferries each way, each day.' Nor did he want to be in Lerwick – 'I've never lived in a town and didn't want to start now' – and he rejected the south mainland of Shetland, 'because that is where all the birders live and I wanted to chart my own course. So I narrowed it down pretty quickly.'

The house that caught his eye when it popped up on the screen of his first home computer – 'a vast grey box that took up half my desk' – was a whitewashed stone cottage. As soon as he saw it, something stirred in his subconscious, a recollection of childhood. 'It resembled, almost exactly, my grandmother's house in Cornwall. She was my special person when I was growing up and her house was my happiest place on earth. So naturally, I couldn't resist it. It was like falling in love at first sight. "Wow!" I thought. "You're the one!"'

It was also in the perfect location for someone with Jon's

exacting requirements. It sits on the ridge on the eastern peninsula of Whalsay, which itself lies a half-hour ferry ride east of the main island – 'So it gets lots of birds. You can also see the sea from the windows. I watch whales while I'm washing up. And the maritime heath on my land is full of very cool flowers. Of course, I didn't see all that when I saw the listing . . .'

Against the advice of his solicitor – and pretty much everyone else – Jon, led entirely by his emotional response to a photograph, went ahead and bought the house. It was spring 2003. He moved up there that autumn, seeing the house for the first time when he went to collect the keys.

Shetland is made up of around a hundred islands, 16 of them inhabited. Whalsay has the biggest population after the main island – roughly a thousand people spread over a little less than 12 square miles of land, although most live near the harbour in the main settlement of Symbister.

Something I've always felt when visiting Shetland – but wasn't sure whether I was being fanciful – is that every island has its own very distinct personality. It's hard to quantify because Shetland hospitality is famous. It was another factor that made the prospect of living here so appealing to Jon. His solitary childhood made him crave being part of a big family but, as he says, family doesn't have to be biological. His idea was to find a 'logical family' based on choice rather than DNA. And the friendliness and openness of the people of Shetland was incredibly attractive. And there is more substance to that hospitality than people being chatty in the shop or waving to you on the road. There is a care and concern for people, even strangers, which is perhaps only possible in small communities.

I once left my purse in the little shop that used to be on the edge of the harbour on the island of Yell. I hadn't even realised I'd left it there until later that evening when I was back on the main island and the friends I'd been visiting called me. The owner of the shop had found my purse, knew I was visiting someone on the island but didn't know how to contact them, so put a message on Facebook. Someone else saw it and phoned my friends, who knew that I was leaving Shetland on the early flight the next morning. The last ferry to Yell had already sailed, so the only way I would get my purse back on time was for them to phone the owner of the shop, an elderly lady who would usually be in bed by this time, and ask her to meet them where the ferry would dock. With minutes to spare, they raced to the shop, got my purse, handed it to the ferry man taking the last ferry of the night back from Yell to the mainland and told me to be there to meet it. I reached the harbour just as the ferry pulled in and was handed a brown envelope with my purse safely tucked inside.

I was overwhelmed by this kindness and collaboration, but everyone I told on Shetland seemed unsurprised. It's just what people do. Wherever you go, you're met with easy-going welcoming informality, but still, there is definitely something – intangible but present – that sets each island apart from the other. Jon concurs. He describes Whalsay as self-reliant and strong and puts that down to it being the fishing capital of Shetland. 'Whalsay men kept fishing, even after fishing in other parts of Shetland had stopped for various reasons, so it has a very strong identity. The people are very independent, families are very close, people keep themselves to themselves. Yet at the same time, there is always the feeling that people have got your back, that someone will always look out for you.'

Can nostalgia make a home?

Perhaps not on its own, but without it, perhaps Jon would never have ended up here. It can be lonely, especially in the winter, out on his peninsula with no immediate neighbours, but he was prepared for that. And he has his animals, his books and the space and wildness he longed for. 'I'm like a hermit crab! I've built my shell around me and it's my home. No one can take it away from me. I've paid off my mortgage. It's MINE! It's safe and I have my Shetland community as family. It's everything I need to make me feel at home.'

So that emotional impulse to buy a house because it reminded him of the only place he felt happy as a child has paid off. He has lived in his whitewashed stone cottage for almost half his life and is so sure he will never leave that he's had it written into his will that he wants to be buried on his land.

The Guillemot

———

It's not just the people of Shetland who are so strongly rooted to their home patch. The birds that nest on the cliffs, that raise their young on the narrow shelves of rock above the dip and swell of the grey-green sea, show a similar doggedness in their loyalty to their islands. This is particularly true of the guillemots.

These sleek little birds have an air of formality about them. The white plumage on their breasts, as crisp and stark as a starched dress shirt, set off by the intense, velvety, dark chocolate feathers on their backs and heads, combine to give the impression they have been dressed by a valet in a morning suit. They nest in proliferation around the coasts of the various islands that make up the Shetland archipelago, but the largest colony is at Sumburgh Head, on the southern tip of the main island. Like many sea birds, they are – mainly – monogamous and return to the same cliffs every year to breed. But guillemots will be the first birds to return after their summer moult at sea, as if they can't bear to be away from their home for too long. And they not only return to the same cliff but to the exact same spot on that cliff.

If you believe in reincarnation, have a hatred of crowds and value personal space, you have to hope that you will not return to earth as a guillemot. They live so tightly packed on their precarious rocky ledges that they are in almost constant contact with the birds on either side of them. Yet, astonishingly, what appears to be an unruly, raucous gathering of unremitting chaos is nothing of the kind. Each shelf is the closely guarded, much-prized nest site for birds that are related to each other. Not only do the same guillemot pair return to the same tiny patch of cliff – a patch just a few centimetres square – every year, but they will somehow squeeze their daughters and other female members of their family onto the same ledge. They will defend it fiercely and their loyalty to it is absolute. But good territory is constantly challenged and if a bird does lose its spot, it won't settle for any old shelf on any old cliff, but will drift for a year or more until the right place on the right cliff comes along. Home, for a guillemot, matters.

Land and Sea

It looks like something from a fairy tale: low rise, half hidden by the hill, its unpainted wooden exterior blending into the landscape. Guided by the plume of smoke rising from the chimney, I have arrived at the cabin on foot, on the advice of Matt who warned me the track was sheet ice. It is. I have followed its upward curve, keeping to the grass alongside it.

It's been below freezing, night and day, for the best part of two weeks. The grass is crisp with frost; my crunching feet leave icy indentations in my wake. The trees are encrusted in white crystals, all glittering in the sun beneath a cloudless sky of unsullied blue. I stop at the foot of the cabin's steps, turn and look back. And gasp. I had had no sense of what was out there when I parked down below, screened in by a thicket of holly and hawthorn and the field's steep, upward curve. The slope I've climbed undulates as it rises and, now that I'm almost at the summit, I can see over the hedges that bisect the fields and look down to where the land ends in an uneven line and gives way to the sea. 'Well of course you'd want to live here!' I say to myself and turn to see Matt at the top of the steps, warning me that 'they're slippery as hell!'

The cabin is warm inside. The door leads straight into the kitchen, a narrow, galley-like space with a wooden picnic table at one end, a small wood burner and a clutter of pans and jars and crockery on shelves. There is a bucket of eggs on the floor and children's drawings on the wall. A handful of winter kale rests on the worktop, clearly just picked, its dark, wrinkled leaves still thickly encased in ice.

A gap in the wall leads to a narrow corridor off which is the children's bedroom, with hand-built bunks, posters and toys, and bright triangles of bunting hanging from the ceiling. The room next to it is full of salvaged building materials and stacks of thick, folded cardboard, and at the end is the bedroom Matt shares with his wife, Charis. It feels like a pioneer's cabin: hand-built, unadorned, practical. Nothing fancy. No mains electricity. No central heating. But there's water in the taps, the fire is lit, the roof is sound. Charis hands me a mug of tea and I follow them both into the horsebox.

Although I would never have guessed from the outside, Matt and Charis built this cabin around the body of a lorry once used to transport horses and two old flatbed trailers that had carried bulk loads of hay and straw, before age and wear and tear made them no longer fit for purpose. It is an ingenious construction. Being raised off the ground has meant no need for damaging foundations or pilings and helps prevent damp. And it was relatively quick and easy to do – which was important as Matt and Charis had nowhere else to live and no experience of building anything.

We push through a thick curtain that leads from the kitchen, through a plywood door and into a cosy den. There's another wood burner, a small sofa and a couple of armchairs, a telly and children's toys in a low stack of baskets. 'That's a lot of dinosaurs,' I laugh, seeing the overflowing jumble of triceratops and diplodocus and T-rex. Of horns and limbs and tails and jaws. The walls of the room are covered entirely by a collage of photographs and pictures of animals. There are shelves of books and what appears to be hundreds of DVDs. 'This is the horsebox,' says Charis. 'We replaced the ramp with big windows.' The giant panes of glass reveal the view and we all fall silent for a moment, gazing out.

'It's pretty good, isn't it?' says Matt, his eyes still fixed on the sea.

'When we came to look at this piece of land, it was that view that decided us,' adds Charis.

So, how did this young couple with their two children come to live in a homemade shack on a hill overlooking the sea? What path did life lead them down to bring them here?

'Shall I start at the beginning?' asks Matt.

'Why not?' I say.

It wasn't a building that made Matt feel at home when he was growing up but his friends. His family had moved to East Anglia when he was six years old, but soon after, his father left, abandoning his wife and three young children. 'So our house was an emotionally traumatic place. Life was very unpredictable; it never felt completely safe. And because my father had chosen to leave us, I thought I was worthless. All my associations with home and with adults were unhappy. The only place I felt at home when I was growing up was out in the woods or on my bike with my friends.'

Matt left straight after he'd taken his A-levels, worked in a hotel during his gap year and then went to university in London to study veterinary medicine. It was the tight-knit community that he became part of there – the camaraderie that comes from being with people all doing the same thing, sharing experiences, worrying together about exams – that made Matt feel, for the first time, part of a family. His years at university gave him the sense of home he'd missed out on while he was growing up. 'So when we had finished our course and everyone went off to do their own thing, I felt like I'd been abandoned all over again. It was ridiculously distressing.'

In an attempt to counteract the trauma he felt, Matt decided to stay on at university, taking a residential internship at the college in the hope of holding on to at least some of the security he felt he'd found. But he ended up being sent to a veterinary practice in Somerset, where he had no friends, no support network and lived a lonely, solitary existence in a poky little bedsit. Perhaps unsurprisingly, he left and drove on a whim to Aberdeen, took a ferry to Iceland and spent two or three months exploring the country, living in his Land Rover. And on that trip, he realised that he didn't want to be detached or rootless. 'I decided I needed a home.'

The answer, he thought, was simple. He'd buy a house and that would be it. He'd have a home. It never occurred to him that the place he'd chosen – in part because it had a mountain behind it and a bit of a view, but mainly because it was cheap – wouldn't automatically and instantly feel like home. The problem was he had no emotional connection or response to the place, and, although he spent a bit of time and money on doing it up, he never really intended to live there, preferring instead to remain a locum, moving from job to job without any ties, too fearful of attachment that, in his experience, only led to abandonment. He made a token effort, a half-hearted attempt to become part of the community, including joining the local rugby club, but he never felt very comfortable there. When a long-term locum job came up at his old university, he rented out his house and moved back to London. 'University was where I had felt part of a family and the only place I had ever really felt at home.' While working as a mentor to a new intake of veterinary students, he met Charis.

Charis had grown up in Hertfordshire, moving, at the age of 15, to the small town where she went to school. The move was exciting more than upsetting, although she had loved the garden at their previous house, where she and her brother would ride up and down on their bikes and climb the oak tree that stood near the end of the lawn. But in the new town she could be more independent, walking to school, and she was closer to where her friends lived. And she was allowed to paint her new bedroom. 'I did it really badly! I picked two colours – two different purples – and painted each wall a different one, except for the final wall, which I painted with both, dividing them with a really dodgy diagonal line. It was pretty awful!'

When she got into veterinary school in London, it was close enough to her house for her to commute in every day – 'But I didn't want to do that. I was ready to be independent, and although I loved both the houses I grew up in, I wanted to distance myself a bit and get out.' She moved into halls and then shared flats with other students until she graduated and qualified. She and Matt got together and when he was offered a job teaching animal welfare at a college in Northamptonshire, she took a job in a nearby practice and went with him. They rented a house together. 'It was tiny!' Charis remembers.

'But cute,' interjects Matt. 'I had this sort of *Country Living* image in my head, so I bought some rustic, chunky wooden furniture in a conscious effort to try to make this place the home I kept searching for but had never found.'

But quickly things started to unravel. The stress of the job and the long hours were taking their toll on Charis. She developed eczema and severe migraines, and eventually had to concede that she couldn't keep going. She would try locum work in the hope that was more manageable. A job came up in Essex, covering sick leave for one of the senior vets. The job came with a house, too, right next door to the practice. For a while, she went back to the house she shared with Matt at weekends, but when it transpired that her job was going to be more long-term, she decided to stay and Matt, once again feeling restless and unhappy with his job, decided to move to Essex with her. The collection of photographs and animal pictures was already established and was transferred to the walls of the Essex house from Northampton, together with the growing library of DVDs.

'Stories and films are a big thing for both of us,' Charis tells me, 'but if Matt really loves a film he needs to watch it over and over again, so he needs to own it.'

'Some of these films are my closest friends,' says Matt. '*Hot Fuzz, Dodgeball, The Incredibles* . . .' And I can see that he's absolutely serious, that his films have been one of the few consistent sources of comfort he's had in his restless quest to find security and contentment. 'They've come with me everywhere, to every place I've lived.'

Their rented house in Essex had a little garden. They kept a couple of chickens and started to grow vegetables – to put down roots. But living right next door to the practice where Charis worked meant the space that should have offered respite and release was constantly intruded on when colleagues needed her advice or input. Matt was struggling too, not just disillusioned with work, but facing wider issues. From his emotionally traumatic childhood days, he'd grown to be suspicious of authority. This is the basis, he feels, of the challenges he later faced when he was working. He found it difficult to respect his superiors because of his inherent inability to trust them. His formative years had embedded within him a deep-rooted belief that authority figures couldn't be relied on and as he got older, that instinct was compounded, making him deeply unhappy. His unhappiness and the mistrust that fuelled it made it hard for him to find a job where he felt at ease, that sat well with his conscience. He was constantly questioning and worrying about everything. Unable to feel settled at work, he was similarly discombobulated at home. His mistrust widened; he felt unease with the financial imperatives that appeared to dictate so many aspects of life. His life had become a constant search, not just for where to live but how to live; to finally find peace and happiness.

The garden in Essex proved to be something of a catalyst. They had never grown anything before but the joy and satisfaction of picking and eating their own crops became addictive. It made them want to try to grow more. It made Matt think that they should buy some land. 'We didn't imagine it being a place to live,' clarifies Charis. 'The thought was that it would be a little place that was ours, not rented, and where we could plant trees and keep bees and grow food.'

'It was somewhere we could centre ourselves on. The place we would go to recover,' Matt adds.

He dreamed of being near the sea, of recapturing a part of his childhood that had been happy, when he had stayed with his grandmother on the Sussex coast. It perhaps would have made sense for them to look in Essex, where they were still living, or even in Sussex, but instead they searched on the opposite side of the country, near where Matt had once worked in a town on the west coast of Wales. He'd often camp out there, he said, rather than stay in the B&B – the accommodation that went with the locum job – loving the sense of peace and liberation he got from looking beyond the confines of the land to the endless possibilities of the sea. The space, he said, made him feel safe.

So they started to search for somewhere that would recapture that feeling. To do that, they felt it needed to be in the same area. Because it was to be a place of retreat rather than somewhere to live, they weren't worried about practicalities like access – the land didn't need to lead directly from a road or a lane – or its aspect, as long as they could see the sea. All they wanted was a water supply; other than that, they could be entirely led by their hearts. If being there felt right, if it was both secluded but not hemmed in, that would clinch it.

It was a February day when they saw this parcel of land for the first time, on the suggestion, almost as an afterthought, of a local estate agent. It was muddy and cold, north facing, but, Matt says, his eyes shining with the memory, 'Amazing!'

'We both just wandered around up here on the top, feeling a bit awestruck,' Charis adds. 'We just loved it.'

They'd been saving money for a deposit to put down on a house. Charis had been offered a permanent position as a senior vet in the practice she'd been a locum for in Essex. She was considering the rootedness and security that comes with a staff job, alongside taking the leap of committing to a mortgage and a house that wasn't rented. But Matt was nervous of being at the mercy of banks and loans. He kicked back against the idea that something as fundamental, as essential as your 'home' can be bought and sold. 'Homes shouldn't be trading commodities. They shouldn't be investment vehicles. They are so much more than that. They mean so much more than that. Nor does home have to be what society has conditioned us to expect: the two-up, two-down house with a front door and a chimney, like children draw at primary school. I felt more at home living in my Land Rover than I did living in the house I grew up in. Home is as much a feeling as it is a place.'

So they spent the money they'd saved for a deposit on a house on the land they'd fallen in love with. They celebrated by camping the night here, next to the stream, drinking beer by a fire, then waking up to the sight of the sea beyond the open flaps of their tent. 'And it felt like home.' Though they knew they couldn't live here. There was no planning permission and they had no money to build even if there was, so they found a compromise. Instead of taking the full-time job Charis had been offered, they left Essex, living in a series of rented houses closer to their land and continued to take locum work. And every spare moment, they came to their hilltop retreat.

But there was a way they could live here. They discovered a Welsh government scheme that would allow the building of a home in open countryside, as long as the strict environmental requirements it set out were met. Not only did the house have to be off-grid, they had to commit to a stringently monitored, low-carbon lifestyle and generate a substantial proportion of their family income from the land itself. For Matt and Charis, this was exactly how they wanted to live, was what they had dreamed of but had never thought possible. They applied and, as soon as permission was granted, they were allowed to live on the land in a temporary structure until such time they could build a house.

They couldn't wait to leave their rented accommodation and, for the very first time in their lives together, live somewhere that was truly theirs. By now they had a daughter, Elsa, who was two. They bought an old horsebox and together they drove up the hill and parked it tucked in the lee of the brow with an uninterrupted view of land, sea and sky. They put a rudimentary kitchen in the back of the lorry – 'It was not more than a plank of wood! And we washed up outside. We had a wood burner and our bath was half a barrel.' They found a cheap caravan to sleep in and, although there was little in the way of traditional comforts, they had no regrets. They had, they realised, never felt so happy.

The birth of their second child meant they needed a bit more space. The straw bale house they had permission to build was not yet financially in reach, so they improvised, buying instead two flatbed trailers that were no longer roadworthy and using them as the basis for their cabin. Neither Matt nor Charis had ever built anything before, so they had to make things up as they went along, try things out, learn by trial and error, through sheer determination and necessity. They weren't too ambitious; they kept things simple and, apart from the electrics, which are powered by solar energy, they did everything themselves, changing and adjusting things as they needed. Because they built it, 'We know every inch of it,' Charis says with justifiable pride, and they both feel more at home here than anywhere they have ever lived.

'It's part of me,' says Matt, his face creasing with emotion. 'It was built from here.' And he pats the left side of his chest, where his heart is.

The Common Wasp

I'm supposed to be cleaning out the hen houses but I'm transfixed by two wasps that have alighted on the door of the shed. The shed is old. We bought it from the local garden centre soon after we moved here. It was an ex-display model going cheap because it was already slightly dilapidated, and its dilapidation has only increased over the years. It's much patched and not completely watertight, but it's still standing. Just. The thin, soft wood used to build it has darkened with age and become even softer, almost spongy, after its many winters enduring frost and rain. And the wasps on the door are scraping at it with their mouthparts, leaving pale streaks where they have stripped away the top layer. They take off, one after the other, and I follow them with my eyes as they fly into the shed and up to the back. That's when I notice the nest, discreetly tucked away in an unlit corner, partially obscured by the bottles and tubs crowded onto the shelf beneath it.

A wasp nest is a thing of beauty: a delicate paper lantern made up of onion skin-like layers protecting hexagonal cells. The building of this nest would have been started by the queen. Back in the spring, when she emerged from hibernation, she would have set about finding what she deemed the perfect location for the colony she would go on to produce. Her requirements are modest and practical: somewhere safe and dry with something structurally strong enough for the nest to be built onto. She might have chosen a crevice within the old stone wall at the back of the flower bed with a view of sunflowers and dahlias and the scent of cat mint. Had I been her, I would have been tempted by the hollow in the apple tree, with its promise of a feast of windfalls in late summer, but I clearly don't think like a queen wasp. Because her waspy brain decided the dark, dank corner in a messy shed, that is opened up and rootled around in twice a day by a human, was The Place to build her home.

Once that was decided, she would have performed a dance in front of the nest site. She wasn't celebrating finding the perfect spot; the dance enabled her to fix the location of the site in her mind, so she could navigate back to it. Because her next task was to set about collecting the material to build the nest itself. And again, her demands were minimal. All she needed to find was some wood. A fence post would do, or the gate that leads into the chicken field. Or the door of the shed. Why travel further than you have to? She set about gathering mouthfuls of thin shavings, methodically scraping them off the door and then mixing them with her saliva to create what is effectively papier-mâché. With this, she began to construct the beginnings of the nest, moulding it from the wood pulp until she had formed enough cells for her to crawl inside and start laying the eggs that were fertilised when she mated before hibernating. She needed a workforce and what better way to ensure dedication and loyalty than to give birth to it yourself?

A little less than a month after she laid her first eggs, the queen's first generation of workers emerged from the nest. Now she could concentrate solely on laying more eggs and producing more wasps because her workers would continue building the nest for her. She lost the ability to fly and would now stay in the nest for the rest of her life. In the meantime, the workers got on with creating enough space for the increasing colony. They laid down a trail of pheromones from the nest which they can follow back, in the manner of Hansel and Gretel, once they have their mouths full.

I continue to watch the wasps on the door, diligently scraping away and then taking flight back to the nest. Over the coming weeks, it will grow to be the size of a misshapen football and come the autumn, the queen will die, having ensured her legacy is continued by a new generation of queens that will leave the nest, mate and then go into hibernation for the winter. The rest of the colony, unable to survive without the queen, will disperse and die, leaving the nest in the corner of my shed as a daily reminder of the architectural beauty a wasp can create with a bit of spit and sawdust.

A Scottish Glen and Pieces of Blanket

———

'It was the springboard that made me say, "Right, world! Come on! Where are you? What's out there?"' Tim Peake is talking about his childhood. He spent the first 18 years of his life in a village not far from Chichester. 'It was a lovely place to grow up. There was plenty of countryside around. Kids in the street to play with. We'd go off on our bikes and play in the woods. We were able to have the freedom that now, as a parent, I don't always feel comfortable giving my own children.'

Childhood holidays were similarly bucolic, although usually spent abroad, in the Ardèche valley in southern France. Tim's parents would take the caravan down, often arranging to meet up with other families who lived on their street, so they brought all the stability – and enjoyment – of home with them. 'Home for me was not so much the bricks and mortar we lived in, but a place of family and a place of friends,' Tim remembers.

His childhood bedroom was the boxroom in the three-bed semi – 'the exact width of a single bed' – and at night he would sit looking out of his window at the stars. 'From an early age I was fascinated by the stars and we often seemed to have lots of lovely clear nights, so I learned the constellations and where to find them in the night sky. And yes, I had Lego space rockets – I think most people my age did then [Tim was born in 1972, not long after Apollo 11's historic moon landing] – but I wasn't one of those little boys who said "I want to be an astronaut when I grow up." I never dreamed of that while I was looking at the stars. I just had a sense of something being out there that needed exploring.'

What Tim did dream of was being a pilot. He did maths, physics and chemistry at A-level – 'Got the stellar result of a C, D and an E' – and decided to join the army. He was told he had a place, but only after he'd had a gap year. 'You're young,' he was told. 'Go and get some experience.' So he worked in a pub to earn the money to join an Operation Raleigh expedition to Alaska.

'It was a real culture shock, to be immersed in a completely different country with incredible landscapes and nature and wildlife, alongside other people from all over the world who had very different backgrounds and upbringings from me. It was a transformative part of my life.' And despite – or perhaps because of – his very anchored childhood, he never felt homesick. 'I was having too much of a good time! It was an incredible three months.'

The closest he has ever felt to the anguish of homesickness came once he joined the army, during his first few weeks at the military academy of Sandhurst. 'It was just horrific. All your comforts are taken away – your personal belongings, your personal space – to make it feel as close as possible to what it is like in prison. That's the job of Sandhurst. To break you down then build you up again to be the physical and psychological ideal they are looking for.'

His teammates got him through it. They could take comfort in the fact that they were all going through the same thing. They'd talk about it with each other and even manage to laugh about it. But during exercises in which they were deprived of any comfort associated with home, of sleep and food, and pushed until they were stressed and exhausted, they had to dig deep, drawing on an inner strength to build up a level of resilience that few of them, Tim included, had ever in their lives had to rely on before.

This was the first step towards realising his childhood dream of becoming a pilot. From Sandhurst, Tim joined the Army Air Corps, but before he was allowed to learn to fly, he was sent to get some experience with the infantry. Aged 20, he found himself the platoon commander in charge of 30 people on patrol in Northern Ireland. It was 1992, before the ceasefire, and although the truly terrible years were in the past, there was still, he says, 'A lot going on. Multiple shootings and bombings. Soldiers were still being killed.'

The home we idealise is a place of refuge and retreat. It is where we go for respite. It is a place of safety, security and happiness. But while on deployment with the armed forces, you don't have a home. You can't go back at the end of the day, open your own front door, hug your family, sit in your favourite chair with your cat on your lap. You can't sink into your own warm, comfortable bed, surrounded by the familiar things – the sounds, the smells that wrap you up in the security blanket of belonging. So where do you find that, when you come in off patrol, after hours of being in a heightened state of alert and awareness, adrenalin coursing through your veins? Where do you go when you're in a place where almost nowhere is safe?

'It's the compound,' says Tim. 'Every time you retreat behind the wire, it's like coming home. Even though it's not a home that anyone would recognise as such, with mortar-proof roofing and metal grills on all the windows, it's still home. It's the place you can go, put your feet up, have a cup of tea and recharge your batteries for the next day.' And when he returned to the officer's mess and found letters waiting for him in the mailbox, they were, Tim says, a really important, wonderful connection to real home life.

The springboard of his stable, loving childhood had catapulted Tim into a very different way of life: the nomadic, rootless existence that goes with being in the army. After he left Northern Ireland, he spent a year doing his pilot's course and then was posted to Germany, Kenya, Canada, Cyprus, Bosnia and back to Northern Ireland. 'But I was a young, single guy flying helicopters. I was exactly where I wanted to be. I wanted to lap it up, enjoy every experience, go to as many places as possible.'

After four years, he became an instructor and then went to North America to fly Apache helicopters with the US Cavalry.

'That was my army career. Just bouncing around all over the place and gradually making my way up the ladder of a professional pilot.' And at no time did he wish to settle. He had no hankerings to find somewhere in the world where he would feel content to stay and that he would call home, he explains. 'I wasn't thinking of any of that. I had no long-term plan. I was just enjoying flying and if anyone tried to pull me out of the cockpit, I'd do whatever it took to be able to jump back in again. It's why, when I came back from the States and the army were finally going to put me behind a desk, I left and became a civilian test pilot.'

But one aspect of his life had changed. On a posting to Germany, he had met Rebecca, who was also in the army. They had married during his first year working in America and she had gone out there to live with him. When they returned to the UK, they did both think they would try and settle down a bit, but it wasn't in either of their natures.

Rebecca's childhood had been the polar opposite of Tim's. She was born in Scotland and her family moved constantly, every two years, following her father's work. They even emigrated to Australia for a time. 'So she's as equally outgoing and adventurous as I am, always looking for new journeys and seeking adventure,' Tim says. 'She's much calmer about our lifestyle than me. I worry about moving our children around so much, when I know how formative those stable childhood years were for me. But her childhood, although completely different from mine, was every bit as happy. So she tells me not to worry, says it's good for the boys, that it introduces them to different cultures and to change.'

On their return from America, Tim and Rebecca lived in army quarters in Larkhill on the edge of Salisbury Plain. They stayed there for seven years, the longest either of them had ever remained in one place during their adult lives. Although, Tim qualifies, for two of those seven years he was working up in Yorkshire and would be away all week, with a tortuous six-hour commute at either end. He has fond memories of being at Larkhill. It was a beautiful area. His morning running route was around Stonehenge and back, and he and Rebecca were enjoying life together as a couple. But still it felt temporary. He didn't feel anchored there. 'And I kind of liked that. I liked the feeling at the time of not being bogged down. I didn't mind not putting down roots.' There was one constant in their lives, however: their furniture, which went wherever they went – 'It was our belongings that gave us a sense of home more than bricks and mortar.'

They left Larkhill because Tim had seen an advert. The European Space Agency (ESA) usually recruited their astronauts by approaching the nations that paid into the ESA programme and asking them to send their selected candidates for training. There were no British astronauts because the UK wasn't a member of the programme. But that year, the ESA decided to change things, to select astronauts from all European member states, whether they paid into the programme or not. It was the first moment Tim was struck with the idea that he could become an astronaut, that the stars outside his boxroom window, which had so entranced and intrigued him as a child, could be within his reach.

The ESA selected him and he, Rebecca and their newborn son Thomas moved to Cologne in Germany for Tim to begin his training. Then it was Bonn. Then Houston. And even though Houston was another temporary stopping place, a place they had to be solely for Tim's training and the lead up to his space mission, he describes it as home. Because during the time he was living there, he was away for months at a time: 'I went to Moscow. I went to Canada. You end up bouncing around on this conveyor belt of a training programme that takes you towards your launch date. I was probably away 50 per cent of the time, so the house in Houston was the only constant. It was home. It was the place I could relax, somewhere I could switch off. It was a lovely house with a swimming pool and our furniture was there! Same sofa. Same coffee table. It all got shipped out in a container. And my family was there. That was the key. So yes, it was home, even though we knew it was always just another temporary place to live.'

A critical component of an astronaut's pre-mission training is the psychological preparation needed to undertake long duration space flight. Tim was going to be away from his family and his home for six months, living on the International Space Station (ISS) with five fellow crew members. He wasn't just leaving Rebecca, Thomas and their youngest, Oliver, for another country, but leaving the planet altogether. It is an extraordinary reality. So, the small, personal belongings the astronauts are able to take with them are an important connection to have.

I tell him I have no concept of what the space station is like, that I imagine it being a bit like one of those strangely anonymous corridors at airports, the ones that run between getting off the plane and passport control, where you have no sense of the outside world, or of time or place. 'Scale down the size a bit,' he says. 'But it's not dissimilar. There's one long, narrow tube that forms the length of the space station, that is not as wide as my ceiling here is high, and there are a few modules going off at tangent angles to that. It's not tiny. About the same internal size as a 747. So you don't feel claustrophobic or cooped up. There's plenty of space for six crew members.'

They each have their own crew quarter, a small private space about the size of a telephone box. 'So my childhood bedroom was perfect training for that, it turns out! It's the tiniest space ever, but it's your space. It's where you can retreat. It's where you can have your privacy and just recharge yourself and I think that if you don't have anywhere like that in your life it probably leads to feelings of instability and insecurity.' This is where Tim kept his family photographs. Rebecca had cut a corner off each of the boys' blankets – Oliver's grey one and Thomas' blue one – which Tim says, smiling at the memory, 'really reminded me of home.' The space station is kept supplied by a cargo vehicle every few months and half a kilo of the weight allowance it can carry is set aside for crew care packages. There had been a delivery just before Tim arrived in the week before Christmas, and awaiting him was a present from Rebecca. It was an advent calendar and behind each door, written on airmail paper, was a letter from a friend or a member of his family.

The space station, he relates, is a very sterile environment to live in. 'It's the same temperature, same humidity, same lighting. Nothing changes. You start to realise how much you miss nature, the changing weather and seasons. And colour. Blue, but particularly green. Green is so important to us as humans, I think, and there's no green on the space station. There was one poster, in the Russian segment, of a green field with some trees in it and at the end of each week, on a Friday night, we'd all go and have a nice crew meal there together. Everyone would end up staring at that poster as if sucking in and absorbing that green colour.'

But he did have a means of escape. The treadmill on board transported him to Glen Artney, in Scotland, and his favourite running route, thanks to an app. The programmers had contacted him before the mission and when he told them his favourite place to run, they recorded the route for him to follow while in space. 'And there I was, on a treadmill, in the most sterile and isolated environment looking at the images on a laptop of a landscape I love, moving with me as I ran.'

Every crew member's favourite place on the space station is at the cupola window. The ISS is oriented in such a way that the Earth is always in sight. And it gives, Tim says, this incredible holistic view of our planet. 'You see it in a completely different way: as a living, dynamic place where everything is connected – global weather systems, the aurora, the Earth's magnetosphere. You see the atmosphere every time the sun rises and sets. You see everything, and all at the same time, not in isolation.

'Space is very intimidating. It's a very hostile place. It's the blackest black you will ever see. There is nothing friendly there. When you are on a spacewalk, it is very serene and rather beautiful, just to float there, looking down on the Earth, but it also makes you realise that we are not designed to be in space or to live there. When you look at the Earth from that perspective, you are struck by the absolute realisation that it is the one cradle of life in the universe that we know of. It is incredibly special. It's so different from Mars, or Venus, or Jupiter, or Saturn. And I realised too, while I was up there, that if anyone had asked me where I was from, I would have pointed at the Earth with my finger and said, "I'm from there. I'm an Earthling. That's home."'

Tim is talking to me from the house that he, Rebecca, Oliver and Tom have lived in for the last 18 months. It's not far from Chichester, not far from where Tim grew up. He has come full circle. And it's theirs. They've bought it. 'It's our first home, really. The first time when I've realised, "Oh god! I've got a mortgage on this place. I can't just cancel the rent!" It's nice on one hand. We wanted to have stability for the children while they are at school, but on the other hand, I've lost that "flighty feeling" of just being able to get up and go. Rebecca's the same as I am. Sometimes, we look at each other and I know we're thinking the same thing: that as soon as the kids are out of school and into university, we're going to sell this place, buy a camper van and go off travelling around the world.'

But as an Earthling, of course, that means Tim won't be leaving home.

The Echidna

Small and spiky, the echidna could be mistaken for a hedgehog, but it's not. It has spines, a long, sensitive snout and can roll up in a ball when threatened, but it also lives in Australia, where there are no hedgehogs, and it lays eggs, despite being a mammal, which hedgehogs definitely do not.

Echidnas lead a largely solitary life. Each animal has its own territory and when it's not out looking for the ants or termites that its snout is so perfectly designed to sniff out, and catching them with its long, sticky tongue, equally perfectly designed for the job, it hides away. Crevices among rocks, rotting logs and old burrows that once belonged to wombats or rabbits all suffice as cool, shady boltholes to while away the heat of the day, safe from the sharp, hungry eyes of predators. So, although not rare, they are shy and rarely seen.

I did see one once. I spotted it at the side of a road we were driving down one morning and let out an involuntary yell. 'STOP THE CAR!!' I leaped out and ran back to see its prickly behind disappearing into the undergrowth. Too excited to think about snakes and anything else deadly that might be lurking in the Australian outback, I followed it, getting down on my hands and knees to crawl in its wake. Eventually – and mercifully – it soon tired of being followed and stopped, curled up tight into a ball and waited, hoping that its pursuer would soon get bored and lose interest. I didn't. I stayed, crouched down, head low, playing chicken with a monotreme.

It twitched. I held my breath. The curl of its body started to relax and slowly, slowly, it untucked its snout from between its front paws and regarded me with its small, black, enquiring eyes. We both stayed unmoving, almost nose to nose, for some moments before it decided that I really wasn't interesting enough, or ant-like enough, to bother with any further and it shuffled off without a backward glance.

An echidna will usually only dig a burrow when they have a youngster to protect. A female will lay one solitary egg which is incubated not in the burrow, but in her pouch. It hatches after about ten days and her offspring, barely the size of a jellybean, suckles from her within the pouch until it is about three months old. This is when the mother will dig a burrow, using her strong front legs and flattened claws to scoop out a safe haven for her youngster. And there it will stay, getting on with the business of growing bigger, developing spines and learning how to feed itself, for the next 12 months.

There is only one other occasion when an echidna might take to digging a refuge and that's when a fire threatens to sweep through its territory. A wildfire can move with terrifying speed, engulfing everything in its path, so when fire threatens an echidna, and there are no hiding places within easy reach, it will dig a scrape, as deep as it can manage before the flames reach it, in which it will lie flat and put itself into a state of torpor. Only once the fire has passed and the ground cooled will it rouse itself, its spines scorched, or sometimes burned almost down to the skin, and rise, phoenix-like, from the scene of destruction.

Memories and Feelings

———

'I packed my bag in the few hours before we left. I didn't want to take time over it. I didn't want to think about it too hard. I just wanted to close my eyes and do it.'

Iryna was born 33 years ago in a small village in Ukraine. Her birth coincided with the time just before the collapse of the Soviet Union and Ukraine declaring its independence. She lived with her parents and grandparents and grew up listening to the stories her grandmothers told of life under Russian rule, hearing how her father's mother was sent to Siberia when she was six years old and her brother was two because her father had written anti-Soviet articles calling for an independent Ukraine. As punishment, his wife and their two children were loaded onto a cargo train and sent thousands of miles away to a Siberian work camp. Many of the people that were travelling with them, both adults and children, didn't survive the journey.

The camp was in a forest. The cold was so extreme that Iryna's grandmother's hair would freeze to the wooden floor she slept on and, in the morning, she would have to prise and tug it free. Her mother was forced to leave her children all day while she was set to work. They had nothing to eat apart from a soup they made with carrot and potato peelings. 'My grandmother would cry when she told us these stories, but for us they were like fairy tales. They told of things that seemed unbelievable, that were so long ago it was impossible to imagine things like that ever being able to happen again.' Her years in that house, full of love, open-hearted kindness and security, were Iryna's foundation for life. The stories of those strong, resilient women her benchmark.

Her parents moved with their children to the city of Ternopil when Iryna was four years old. It was the first time she'd had children of her own age around her, so any impact of the move was cushioned by making her first friends. Later, when she was in her early teens, her parents moved again to another part of the city and this time the adjustment was harder. She had to go to a different school and try to make new friends. Comfort came from an old wooden pyramid and a doll that had belonged to her grandmother. It was the anchor to her old life, a familiar reassurance when everything else was unfamiliar.

After studying economics at university, Iryna moved to the city of Lviv and took a job with a large retail company. Her generation was the first to be allowed to travel freely. 'Our parents grew up in a closed country. It was very difficult for them to imagine ever going abroad, to travel or to visit people. It was forbidden for ordinary people. But when my friends and I were growing up, we had the internet, we had magazines, we could find out about other countries. We could dream of going travelling to places like Africa or Australia.'

She planned to take a new job in Kyiv, Ukraine's capital city, but she met the man who was to become the father of her daughter, Elif, and moved with him to his home city of Istanbul. It was her first time out of Ukraine and although there were many things that she loved and admired about Turkey, some aspects of life there made her feel uncomfortable. 'As a tourist, the culture, history and architecture of Turkey is wonderful and Istanbul is an amazing city. But when you live there it is different.' She struggled with the restrictions of the religion and with the general attitude towards women. 'Many of the older generation of women can't read or write because their parents wouldn't let them go to school, even just to learn the most elementary things. There's also a perception, particularly among men, that European and Slavic women are "easy to get".' So although people were outwardly hospitable, she couldn't escape the uncomfortable undertones of discrimination and prejudice and that meant, for her, Turkey could never be home.

The couple separated and she returned to Ukraine. 'And I had to rebuild my life from zero, from the beginning again. I had to look after my child and find work.' So she moved back in with her parents, returning to her childhood bedroom in her childhood home. 'I tried to make it feel like mine again, with my favourite stuff. I don't like clutter but I had candles and my collection of magazines. But even though my parents were incredibly kind and such a help looking after Elif, when you've been used to living in your own way it is difficult to go back to living in someone else's house.' Work helped her find her identity again. She got a job in the studio showroom of a local fashion designer. She planned, once she'd been able to save some money, to rent an apartment of her own and she and her colleague at the showroom talked about going into business together.

But then, the unimaginable happened. It started with a prickling sense of unease – an instinct almost – that something unseen and malevolent was gathering momentum. Muttered rumours fuelled niggling worries. Nerves became taut. The air charged with tension. Yet Iryna and her friends brushed away the idea that was now being talked about as a certainty: war was coming.

'We thought it just couldn't happen. It was impossible. We live in the modern world. We don't worry about war; we worry about health and ecology and how to save our planet. We discuss technology and innovation, debate issues around mental health, gender equality, how to live well, the importance of kindness. And we live in an independent country that is part of Europe. No one can declare war on us.'

But a friend in Kyiv told her that she had packed all the things that were important to her in a bag. ' "If something happens, it is waiting. It is ready." I told her no! Unpack the bag! Don't prepare for the worst. It won't happen. Because your brain just can't accept that tomorrow we will be at war. It's impossible. And I remember, very early the next morning, everyone was calling each other and talking of war and bombing, and yet still you don't want to believe it. Still you question whether it can possibly be happening, even as fighter planes were flying over the city. And I will never forget the feeling. The realisation that we were at war. I think I will carry that feeling with me for the rest of my life. I think we all will. And we will never take peace for granted again.'

When the air raid sirens sounded on the first night of the war, Iryna says they didn't really understand what was happening. They weren't prepared at all and they didn't know where to go. 'Elif was asleep and I remember sitting on the floor by her bed thinking, "What do I do? It's dark. It's winter . . ." Can you imagine it?'

'No,' I say.

There were no purpose-built air raid shelters. The government advice was to go to the basement of their apartment building. It's a tiny space, says Iryna, far too small for all the residents living on the ten floors above, and when those first sirens went off, people crowded in with their children and their animals – 'They came with their dogs and cats. Some had small mice or birds. They thought they might never be able to go back to their homes. That they would be destroyed.' Iryna only went to the shelter once. It was very, very cold. People sat in catatonic silence. Or talked manically. Or cried. So the next time she heard the siren, she and Elif stayed in their apartment. It was on the first floor – just as safe as the basement, she reasoned – and followed government advice to lie down on the floor in the middle of her flat, away from the windows and outside walls.

Her city of Ternopil was lucky, she says. It wasn't yet being targeted by missiles but no one knew if or when that was going to happen. Russian forces were attacking Kyiv and who was to guess which city they would attack next. But Iryna felt she had to leave, to take her daughter to the kindest, safest place she knew: back to the village and her grandmother's house. Her parents decided to stay in Ternopil. 'Having never travelled, having never been allowed to travel, it is something they have no wish to do. Even in the places that were being occupied, where terrible things were happening, people of my parents' generation and older were too scared to leave their homes because they think that if they leave, they will lose everything. Not just their home but their identity, the place they belong.'

Before she left, Iryna packed up some old plates and cups that she remembered from her childhood. They weren't being used anymore and were tucked away at the back of a cupboard, so she took them with her. 'I had this strong urge to have something from my past. I like modern things but I also like having things around me that are uniquely connected to me. And I thought, "When this war is over, when I have my own home again, I would like these things to be there."'

The move to her grandparents' village was the right thing to do for Elif, she knew. It was safer and close to the Polish border, offering a chance of escape if they needed to. But once there, Iryna felt very cut off. And she felt guilty. Friends in other parts of Ukraine were being bombed, were losing their homes. Others were volunteering to help the war effort, doing everything from making camouflage nets to cooking for the soldiers. So after just three weeks, she returned with her daughter to Ternopil.

As more and more people became displaced, Iryna became part of a network who would use their contacts, use social media, to help find ways for them to escape: people to drive them, places for them to go. The network would also get them basic necessities like clothes. 'It became my whole focus. I didn't and couldn't think about anything else. It helped me survive.' She and her friends understood too the importance of telling people outside Ukraine the reality of what was happening. 'I told my friends in other parts of Europe: "This really is war. It's not a joke. It's a real, horrible, terrible war." We needed people to pay attention to us, not ignore what was happening because they think Ukraine is backward and insignificant. We needed their help to stop this. We weren't just losing our homes. We were losing our homeland.'

Three or four months into the war, a strange new normal settled over the country. The government was encouraging businesses to re-open, if they could, and people to go back to work, in an effort to keep the economy alive. Elif went to kindergarten while Iryna worked in the office of a retailer in a shopping centre. One lunchtime, the air raid siren went off. Just a few weeks before, a shopping centre in the city of Kremenchuk had been bombed, killing at least 20 people. Many more were injured or missing. As she ran out of the building, Iryna heard the whistling rush of a missile and saw it pass overhead. And all she could think was that her daughter wasn't with her. That there was nothing she could do to protect her. And although their city wasn't considered dangerous, it was, at that moment, when she heard and saw the missile, that she realised nowhere was safe. That she couldn't live with the fear that something might happen to Elif. Or that her child would grow up with war as her normality, asking, as she had a few days before, why new apartment blocks had been built when they would only be destroyed by bombs.

'But I didn't want to leave,' she tells me. 'Even when I had made the decision, I kept questioning it. Kept thinking I have to stay. I have to stay. I felt like a betrayer. I was thinking about myself when I should have been thinking about my country.'

It took over three months for the paperwork she needed to be completed and sent through. Over those months, the reality of her decision started to sink in. 'When you are in your home country, you know lots of people. You have a connection; people know who you are. But when you leave, when you are a refugee in a country where you know nobody, when you have *nothing*, you have to start with nothing.'

She arrived in the UK with her daughter and two suitcases. She brought only clothes and the toy Elif takes with her to bed. She packed nothing of sentimental value because she feared having them here, seeing them every day would be too painful a reminder. It would make her too sad. The Ukrainian word for this feeling is *tuha*. It is the same as *hiraeth*. 'The special things I brought inside me – feelings and memories. Because if you bring with you good memories and good feelings about something, you will never lose them and they will always be there when you need them. When you are reliant on people and stuff it is painful to leave them. This way, I can leave more easily. It helps me feel positive rather than sad.'

She is staying in a cottage deep in the countryside, sharing with another Ukrainian woman who also has a daughter. The owners of the cottage live next door and are, Iryna says, 'Amazing! They have helped me so much. And I said to my friends when I got here "Why do people want to help us? Why do they open up their houses to strangers? It is overwhelming. It is difficult to understand."'

To leave her country for an uncertain future was the hardest decision Iryna has ever had to make but she doesn't regret it. She gets frustrated that she doesn't yet speak English well enough to be able to communicate the way she is used to, yet it is obvious, even in a language not her own, that she is a highly articulate, curious, thoughtful and insightful woman. As well as learning a new language, she is learning to drive. It's challenging – all of it – but she knows she has to make every effort to make the life she has to live, for the time being, work. 'I have to turn this into a positive experience. Life is going on. You have to keep living. You have to embrace it, wherever you are.'

The war, and the pandemic that immediately preceeded it, have taught her that you never know what might happen tomorrow, that nothing is certain: 'Love your home. Love your country. Love your friends. But don't be reliant on any of those things.' Home, she has learned in these last turbulent months, can't always be a fixed point – it can't be a place, a building or a community. That unquantifiable feeling of home has to be inside you, has to be able to be carried with you, so that even when you become rootless, when the foundations of where you belong have gone, you can still survive. Iryna now believes that, 'If you haven't got your home inside you wherever you go, you will not be happy.'

I'm Here

Darkness is coming. We're on top of the hill, heading west, towards the last light of the setting sun. It is disappearing quietly tonight, slipping away without drama. There's no fanfare. No going out in a gaudy blaze of orange and red. Just pale, careless streaks of silver-gold light in a silver-grey sky.

As daylight fades, the landscape becomes gauzy and indistinct. The wide, slow river far below merges into the horizon. Water and sky become one infinite space. The last few wood pigeons hurry to their roost in the trees, their silhouettes, sharp and black, and the flap of their wings loud and urgent against the silence. We should maybe have taken the first path that leads down off the hill instead of pressing onwards, but I love this time, love being witness to the scene change between day and night. It is a thoughtful time. One of contemplation. Of reflection.

It is over two decades since we moved into our second house. I tried so hard to love it. We made endless small adjustments; there was rarely a time when there wasn't some sort of building work going on, some form of disruption, the air heavy with dust, tester patches of colour on cupboard doors or walls. Furniture was re-arranged and pictures moved. Cushions were added, a new rug on the sitting room floor.

The wasteland became a garden. We cleared the nettles, the broken slabs, the collapsing remnants of a shed quietly rotting in the corner. We built a pond, planted shrubs and bulbs, trained clematis and roses up the fences. Heavy glass sliding doors opened from the kitchen onto a terrace with a table and chairs. It faced south and was full of sun. It was overlooked by the line of houses immediately behind but we all overlooked each other. That's city living.

Later, we added a building that spanned the width of the garden and was tucked up hard against the brick wall at the back. It had a living roof: a sprouting thatch of sedum where bees hummed and foraged in the summer. One half of the building was a storeroom – a safe place for bikes, tents and camping kit, orderly racks of labelled boxes. The other half was my office: a garden sanctuary away from the distractions of the house.

We often had friends to stay, invited people for cosy kitchen suppers and lazy, boozy Sunday lunches. It was a good space for parties, as we discovered when we decided to have a 'February Blues' party – an effort to do something cheerful at an often cheerless time of year. We set the date for a Thursday, I remember. A sort of come-after-work-for-a-few-drinks-and-push-off-at-nine kind of affair. We invited lots of people, reasoning that lots of people wouldn't come or would only stay for a bit. What we hadn't taken into account was that few of our friends had had children at that point. And not much happens on Thursday evenings in February. So everyone came.

The house was rammed. People in every room, conversations on the stairs and on the landing. Empty bottles piling up in a corner of the kitchen. I'd made food – the usual party fodder of dips and sausages on sticks – and had worried that I might have over-catered, but found myself rummaging in cupboards and pointing people towards the toaster. There was music and an attempt at dancing, without really the space to do it. Later, the guitars came out. By then, people were slumped on the sofas or sitting in huddles on the floor and up the stairs. There were mildly drunken renditions of Bob Dylan songs and Simon & Garfunkel, trying – and failing – to remember all the words to *The Boxer*, only confident when it came to the *la-li-lies*. The last person left at four in the morning.

It was a house that played host to many happy gatherings. And everyone loved it, making admiring comments about the clever use of space, the internal glass, the bookshelves built into the side of the staircase, the sleek limestone fireplace, the light. Everyone loved it. Apart from me.

In retrospect, I don't think it was the house that was at fault. It was my expectations of it that were unrealistic. Because I didn't just want it to be a welcoming space for our friends and a private, secluded retreat during the times when privacy and seclusion are what's needed. I expected it – wanted it desperately – to be able to fool me into believing that I belonged in the city that was outside its front door. That the city, as well as the house, was my home. And it couldn't. No house, in any part of London, would have been able to do that. So I tried to be away as much as possible, hoping that absence would make my heart grow fonder.

My job made that easy. I was often on work trips for weeks, sometimes months, with only short stints back in London before going away again. And if there was a chance of staying on after we'd finished a job, or going out earlier, I would. Although our work patterns as freelancers were irregular and unpredictable, Ludo and I were generally busy in the spring, summer and early autumn, and there was less – if any – work in the winter. So that was when we'd plan to take our holidays. We discovered that if we travelled no later than mid-December and returned in mid-February, we'd miss the big Christmas price hike. And the worst of the British winter.

We would lend our house to friends nearby while we were away. Their family lived abroad and would visit every Christmas, but space was tight. Someone would always have to sleep on the floor and someone else on the sofa. We could offer a perfect solution that worked equally well for us. We'd pack our camping gear into rucksacks and set off for two months of adventure, knowing our house was being well looked after in our absence. We explored the Atlas Mountains of Morocco. We hiked a little-known route through the forests of Venezuela. We visited friends in Nepal. We returned to Africa. And each time we came back to London, each time we walked through our front door, I would stand for a moment, willing myself to feel that small jolt of joy that nudges your heart when you return to the comforting familiarity of the place that is your home. But I never did feel it. I was, it was clear, tired of London. But not, whatever Samuel Johnson says, tired of life. Just of living in a place I didn't belong.

We had stayed in our first house for seven years. Now the itch got its way again, driving us to leave our second house after trying, and failing, for another seven years, to make it home. In a quest to find a place I felt I belonged, it seemed contrary to settle on somewhere neither of us had a single emotional or physical connection to. But when we had driven our urban Mini west, crossing the River Severn and the border into Wales, my heart gave that jolt. I looked out through the windscreen, over the racing, rippling water to the green hills beyond, and had the inexplicable feeling that I was coming home.

We turned up a dusty stone track, cautiously easing our low-slung car over the ruts and bumps. Trees towered alongside, pressing in, their branches arcing overhead in a rustling tunnel of green. We switchbacked, winding up and up until we were clear of the trees and back into the sunlight. I brought the car to a stop, slightly breathless. We opened the doors and climbed out. Silent, we walked to the edge of a bank overlooking the steep slope of a field that tumbled towards the trees below. Our eyes travelled over the canopy of leaves to the forested ridge on the other side of a narrow valley, over a rolling panorama of fields and hills, rising and falling to meet the sinuous path of the unseen river, and up to another treecovered ridge, a solid, mighty presence, dominating the skyline. Behind us was a house, built several centuries before, solid old stone tucked into the summit of the hill. We had barely glanced at it. Because we knew, instinctively, that this was the place. We had found it. 'Can you ever imagine ever living anywhere other than here?' I asked Ludo. Wordlessly, he shook his head.

And here we are, 15 years later, feeling no itch to scratch. But there is a conundrum to muddle over instead. I want to build a house. It's a desire fuelled by curiosity, rather than necessity, although, in time, that will change. I'm of an age when our parents' generation is dealing with the realities and decisions no one wants to face. The time when it starts to dawn that the place that is their home, that might have been their home for decades, is becoming less a place of refuge and comfort and more a burden and a worry. But if the place that has been your home for so long suddenly isn't, what is? And where is it?

When my own mother was faced with this a few years after my father died, it was traumatic, both for her and, in some ways, for us. For although neither my brother nor I had lived in the house where she and my dad lived for over 30 years, we understood her deep emotional connection to it, to the things in it, to the people around it. We didn't want to be the ones to urge her to look at the realities: the house was old; there was a list of expensive repairs that, although not urgent, soon would be. And it was a family-sized house, too big and too much work for someone on their own. The garden was steep, the stairs steeper, the floor at the bottom of them unyielding stone. And although fit and remarkably spry, she had fallen. Bashed her head and cracked her collar bone. It was a shock to a woman who is fiercely independent and capable, and a shock to her children too. A sharp prod to remind us that although she has never allowed herself to give in to the irritants of becoming older, sometimes age reminds us that no one is infallible.

She sold the house and many of its contents, a wrench she hid with her customary fortitude, although it was still painfully obvious to all who love her that this latest loss was almost as unbearable as the loss of my father. It was the final full stop that marked the end of a life together that had spanned over half a century. But she was unshakeably clear about what she needed to make a new home. It must be bright and light and warm, with an open fire and space for the table she will never part with. Two bedrooms, so people could still come and stay. She wanted a little courtyard garden to fill with pots of flowers. For a few nerve-racking months after she had accepted the offer on her house, nothing suitable came on the market. She had to rent a temporary stopgap and hated the feeling of being unable to settle. But then she phoned me and asked me to come to see a place that she thought sounded perfect.

It felt oddly, comfortingly familiar when I walked through the little courtyard to her front door just a few weeks after she'd moved in. There were already pots and tubs of flowers. A table and chairs. A wooden bench against a sunny wall. Inside, the paintings and the ornaments that I remember always being in our home, were there. She had softened what was a rather stark, white interior with sisal flooring and blinds at the windows. There was a thick, warm carpet, heavy, lined curtains in pretty fabrics and the walls had been painted the same warm, pale yellow that covered the walls of her old house.

But what makes this house home for my mum is not so much the familiar things – photographs, the little desk she was given by her mother, the beloved table – but the familiar people. Because this house is two minutes up the hill from her old house. She is surrounded still by the friends and neighbours she has known for years, who she treasures above all else. They have made her new house her home.

The day will come when we too have to accept that the old stone house and its four acres of land, which we realised as soon as we saw them was where we belonged, that we love with a fierce, territorial force, is too much for us to deal with. And rather than go through the heartbreak of hanging on until all choices we may have had are lost, my instinct is to build a place that fits us, rather than the other way around. That way – by moving before we have to, by choice, rather than from necessity – I hope we will deflect the worst of the pain.

The house is in my head. I've walked through it in my imagination countless times, honing the details as I go. It's not big. Single storey, two bedrooms. A pantry and – crucially – a boot room. A kitchen and sitting room, built around a courtyard so that all the rooms can be opened up to the outside. The courtyard will be our vegetable garden. We'll have a beehive and fruit trees and a pond. The house will be off-grid, built with straw or hemp and lime. We'll have our books, some of the things we've collected on our travels, the cartoon that hangs above the kettle in our kitchen which makes us laugh every time we make a cup of tea. And dogs.

But there's one question that looms large. Leaving aside the unknowables of planning regulations – this is all in my head, where no planning permission is needed – we have the great luxury of being unfettered by anything. We could go anywhere in the world. But that's when we pull ourselves up short and ponder what it is that makes a home. Not just a home – our home. I'm mindful of the lesson we learned with our second house – that despite valiant attempts to turn it into something we truly believed would be perfect, it turned out not to be. And also of the discovery that *where* we live is more critical to feeling at home than the building itself.

Dogs and I scramble over the wall, the dogs with rather more elegance than me, leaving the open hillside and plunging into the woods. It's darker here, the sky obscured by the branches overhead. We weave our way on the narrow path between the trunks, brushing past leafy ferns and the snagging tug of bramble. We reach the point where the path meets a wider track.

A few months previously, I was walking here on a Sunday morning. It was early, the sun still low on the horizon. I was coming from the other way, a steep rough climb, the dogs leaving me in their wake. I heard the faint swish of bicycle tyres on gravel and then voices, distant and indistinct. The dogs barking. I sped up, hoping bikers and dogs weren't getting entangled. The voices became clearer. 'Oh, these will be Kate's,' one said. 'No one else would be out walking this early on a Sunday!'

I smiled to myself, not just because I recognised the voice of a friend, but with the pleasure of being known without even being seen. Of being somewhere where you are so familiar, the people around you know you like to walk early. Where the postman asks after your mum. Where the man in the garage at the bottom of the hill will come and rescue you when the car breaks down. Where neighbours can and do phone each other for help with everything from trees blocking the lane, to lost sheep, to the loan of heaters when boilers break down.

I lost a pig once. She broke out of her field and went for a gallivant in the neighbouring woods. Frantic, I followed her tracks, evidence of a joyful, rooting rampage, but she was nowhere in sight. 'Have you seen my pig?' I gasped, breathless, to John, who lives on the opposite side of the wood and was in his garden, wielding an ancient scythe. His quizzical eyebrows raised enough to clear his impressively bushy beard. 'Big? Ginger? Black spots? Called Dahlia...'

John shook his head. 'I'll go this way,' he said without hesitation, 'and 'I'll call you if I find her.'

I ran back up the lane towards our house, planning to get the car and search the forestry tracks. As I neared the top, I spotted a large, orange rump disappearing around the corner towards the yard. By the time I'd caught up with my errant pig, she was settling down in her favourite muddy patch of field for a bit of a nap. I called John to let him know. 'Just shout if it happens again and I'll keep an eye out,' he said.

Dogs and I follow the track. I glimpse shadowy figures of deer, the white of their tails giving them away before they slip into the cover of the trees. A pair of tawny owls call to each other. I pause to listen. It's a sound I love for its association with these woods that are my patch. Darkness has come, wrapping us up in its inky cloak. The first stars appear. Tiny pinpricks of light. We're still a good half-mile from the house but it doesn't matter. I know where I am.

I'm here.

I'm home.

Author's Acknowledgements

——

Thanks, as ever, goes to Rosemary Scoular of United Agents, for her seemingly bottomless well of encouragement, support and kindness. The same can be said of my Octopus publishing family, as I now regard them: Stephanie Jackson, Caroline Brown, Megan Brown, Charlotte Sanders, Jonathan Christie, Alex Stetter and Constance Lam. Thank you for your continued belief in my middle-of-the-night ideas and for everything you do to help them take shape.

Thank you to Andrew Lee for advice on background research and Emma Ponting for robust but encouraging early feedback. And to Melanie Lewis for her beautiful artwork on the cover.

To all the people who did me the great honour and courtesy of inviting me over their thresholds and into their homes, this book is testimony to your generosity and trust. Thank you all.

And to Ludo, my friends and my animals, all of whom make the impossible possible. You are my home.

Publisher's Acknowledgements

Grateful acknowledgement is made to the copyright holders of the excerpts used on the following pages:

p75: 'DON'T FENCE ME IN', Words and Music by Cole Porter © 1944 WC Music Corp. (ASCAP) All rights administered by WARNER CHAPPELL NORTH AMERICA LTD.

p177: 'Home' from *Bless the Daughter Raised by a Voice in Her Head* by Warsan Shire, published by Chatto & Windus. Copyright © Warsan Shire, 2022. Reprinted by permission of The Random House Group Limited.

p213: 'The Wrong House' from *When We Were Very Young* by A A Milne. Copyright © Pooh Properties Trust 1924. Reproduced with permission from Curtis Brown Group Ltd on behalf of The Pooh Properties Trust.

About the Author

Kate Humble is a broadcaster and author of five books, including *Thinking On My Feet, A Year of Living Simply* and *Home Cooked*. A champion of the environment, nature conservation and rural affairs, she is president of the Wildfowl & Wetlands Trust and founded Humble by Nature, a rural skills centre on her farm in Wales. She lives with her husband and other assorted animals on a smallholding in the Wye Valley.

www.katehumble.com

@kmhumble